A SMALL G

The Five Doors of the Heart

Teaching Children Biblical Purity Basics

Jennie Bishop

w | warnerpress

Warner Press, Inc

Warner Press and Warner Press logo are trademarks of Warner Press, Inc

The Five Doors of the Heart: Teaching Children Biblical Purity Basics

Written by Jennie Bishop

Text Copyright ©2017 Jennie Bishop

Cover and layout copyright ©2017 Warner Press, Inc

Scripture quotations used in this book were taken from the following:

(ESV)	*ESV® Bible* (*The Holy Bible, English Standard Version®*), copyright © 2001 by Crossway Bibles, a publishing ministry of Good News Publishers. Used by permission. All rights reserved.
(NASB)	*New American Standard Bible®* (NASB), Copyright © 1960, 1962, 1963, 1968, 1971, 1972, 1973, 1975, 1977, 1995 by The Lockman Foundation. Used by permission. www.Lockman.org
(NIV)	HOLY BIBLE, NEW INTERNATIONAL VERSION®.*NIV*®. Copyright © 1973, 1978, 1984, 2011 by Biblica, Inc.®. Used by permission. All rights reserved worldwide.
(NIV1984)	HOLY BIBLE, NEW INTERNATIONAL VERSION®. *NIV*®. Copyright © 1973, 1978, 1984 by International Bible Society. Used by permission of Zondervan Publishing House. All rights reserved.
(NKJV)	*New King James Version*®. Copyright © 1982 by Thomas Nelson. Used by permission. All rights reserved.

All rights reserved. No part of this publication may be reproduced, stored in a retrieval system, or transmitted in any form or by any means—electronic, mechanical, photocopy, recording, or any other—except for brief quotations in printed reviews, without the prior permission of the publisher.

Requests for permissions should be sent to:

Warner Press, Inc
2902 Enterprise Drive
Anderson, IN 46013

editors@warnerpress.org

Editors: Robin Fogle and Tammy Tilley

.

Cover: Curtis Corzine

Designer: Katie Miller

ISBN: 978-1-59317-999-1

This book is also available in e-book format.

Printed in USA

A Note to the Reader:

Optimally, this book is intended for parents to study in a group setting, as they learn and teach their children ages 6–8 at home. Parents may also use this guide to study the topic individually if they prefer.

To get the most out of this study, we recommend that you consider purchasing:

The Five Doors of the Heart: Teaching Children Biblical Purity Basics
Leader's Guide
ISBN: 9781593179984
EBook Edition: 9781684340316

The Five Doors of the Heart Introductory DVD
UPC: 730817357973

The Five Doors of the Heart Video Session Digital Download
UPC: 730817357973D

Includes 7 brief introductory videos with author Jennie Bishop, to be used in conjunction with each weekly group meeting.

The Princess and the Kiss™ Storybook
Hardcover with DVD   ISBN: 9781593173807
Softcover   ISBN: 9781684340002
Softcover Spanish   ISBN: 9781593177225

The Squire and the Scroll® Storybook
Hardcover with DVD   ISBN: 9781593173821
Softcover   ISBN: 9781684340019
Softcover Spanish   ISBN: 9781593177232

FREE downloadable parent/child activities pages at: fivedoors.warnerpress.org

To order, visit warnerpress.org.

About the Author:

Jennie Bishop has been studying the subject of purity for more than 15 years. After graduating from a Bible college, then becoming a wife and mother, she recognized a passion for pure hearts that led to an international ministry. Bishop's first three books, *The Princess and the Kiss, The Squire and the Scroll* (both children's books), and *Planned Purity for Parents*, quickly generated requests for her to hold conferences. To date, the author has traveled to Ukraine, Namibia, Nigeria, the Dominican Republic, El Salvador, and Nicaragua, as well as throughout much of North America, to present biblical concepts on purity of heart and body.

Visit Jennie's website: purityworks.org

Or follow her on:
www.facebook.com/PurityWorks
www.twitter.com/jennielbishop

TABLE OF CONTENTS

Introduction 7
The Purpose of the Five Doors of the Heart 9
The Planned Purity® Blueprint 11
How to Use This Book 13
Week 1—*Purity: Guarding the Five Doors of the Heart* 17
    A Lesson with Your Child 22
    1.1 Devotion: Pure Hearts See God 26
    1.2 Devotion: Above All Else 27
    1.3 Devotion: Absolute Purity 28
    1.4 Devotion: Inside Out 29
    1.5 Devotion: Real Love 30

Week 2—*The Door of the Eyes* 33
    A Lesson with Your Child 36
    2.1 Devotion: God Sees 38
    2.2 Devotion: Deadly Invisibles 39
    2.3 Devotion: Outward Appearances 40
    2.4 Devotion: Fire Prevention 41
    2.5 Devotion: Truth That Transforms 42

Week 3—*The Door of the Ears* 43
    A Lesson with Your Child 46
    3.1 Devotion: Music to the Ears 49
    3.2 Devotion: Sermon Stillness 50
    3.3 Devotion: Hearing God's Voice 51
    3.4 Devotion: No Storm Too Big 52
    3.5 Devotion: The Gift of Listening 53

Week 4—*The Door of the Breath* 55
    A Lesson with Your Child 58
    4.1 Devotion: God's Breath 61
    4.2 Devotion: Everything That Has Breath 62
    4.3 Devotion: Something Smells Good 63
    4.4 Devotion: A "To-Love" List 64
    4.5 Devotion: Dry Bones Live! 65

Week 5—*The Door of the Mouth* 67
    A Lesson with Your Child 70
    5.1 Devotion: The Swinging Door 73
    5.2 Devotion: One Way 74
    5.3 Devotion: The Voice of God 75
    5.4 Devotion: Seasoned with Salt 76
    5.5 Devotion: A Spotless Vocabulary 77

Week 6—*The Door of the Skin* 79
    A Lesson with Your Child 82
    6.1 Devotion: Physical Praise 85
    6.2 Devotion: Open Arms 86
    6.3 Devotion: God's Righteous Hand 87
    6.4 Devotion: Hardworking Hands 88
    6.5 Devotion: Hands That God Loves 89

Technology Agreement Sample 91

Introduction

When my daughter was six years old, she came home from kindergarten one day and announced, "I need a boyfriend!" At that moment, I recognized I needed to pray and seek God for my kids' purity.

My prayers that night resulted in a storybook called *The Princess and the Kiss*, in which a princess saves her kiss for a prince.

This story about "waiting" and "saving" that was innocent enough for young children brought a flurry of needy parents who were very concerned about their kids saving sex for marriage. But the more I studied the Bible and spoke on the topic of purity, the more I recognized that purity wasn't about sex—it was about the heart.

With the clamor to write a similar book for boys, I decided to write a story based on what I've called the Five Doors of the Heart, taken from Proverbs 4:20-27 where we are charged to guard the heart above all else. The Squire in *The Squire and the Scroll* retrieves the Lantern of Purest Light for his kingdom by completing five quests based on the doors. This storybook became the primer for purity in young hearts, focusing on the five doors of the senses and the need to guard them to keep the heart pure.

Many years have passed since my daughter's kindergarten announcement, and since then, the challenge to help our children live in purity grows increasingly difficult.

As parents, we have our own family stories that reflect those challenges. That's why this six-week small group study has been created—for you, the parents, to come together in the power, purpose, and presence of God to encourage, support, and share in the battle for our children's hearts toward purity.

As we share openly and honestly with other parents who, like you, seek God's absolute best for our children, please cultivate a sacred space of confidentiality and safety. It is only when we feel safe that we can let down our guard, be vulnerable, and share openly about our struggles.

The small group setting will provide a great way for you to expand the culture of virtue that your family needs to pursue purity successfully. Sharing your struggles in community with others who have the same goal will make for some terrific conversation and opportunities to discover what is working or not working for you. So much happens when we just talk about it!

Remember, the ultimate goal of pursuing purity is to be able to *see God* (Matthew 5:8). That is my prayer for all of us—that as we guard the doors of our hearts, we may see Him, love Him, and live for Him by loving others.

>In Christ,
>Jennie

The Purpose of *The Five Doors of the Heart*

The Five Doors are one element of a purity blueprint I share in the book *Planned Purity for Parents*, where I explain a diagram that shows how purity is successfully pursued at all ages, starting with the heart.

In this study on the Five Doors, my hope is that I can pass on what I've learned from much research and interaction with parents. I'm praying this study will increase your hunger to teach your children purity, not just sexually but even more deeply, at a heart level. When a child's heart is pure, everything else follows. This study is designed to grow your confidence and give you the tools to build the foundational understanding of purity that sexual purity training rests on, the foundation that is often missed because we're so anxious about growing kids in a hyper-sexualized culture.

Instead of wondering about whether you and your children are doing anything to stay pure, the Five Doors will give you a practical assessment tool that keeps you on a consistent path towards purity as you continue to guide and correct your family's course. You will learn to build a strong foundation in your young children that sets them up for an understanding and embrace of sexual purity as they grow. Fear will dissipate as you walk through this program and sensitize yourself to what's needed on a daily basis. And because the pure in heart see God, you are going to see Him at work, and your children will, too!

Maybe you're worried because you already recognize issues with purity in you, your spouse, or your children. You're not alone. These issues are very real, and you couldn't be in a better place than this study to start to figure out how to face them and begin to take back ground as you allow God to work.

Maybe you already feel like you've waited too long to begin these discussions with your child. Remember, we're not necessarily giving you the words to talk about sexuality. We're building the *foundation* for those discussions. If you are already concerned with your child's behavior, you may be heading back to square one and replacing the foundation of what purity is altogether, which will provide so many opportunities for conversations about the issues in question as you work through these lessons. As you ask the Lord to lead you, He will!

As the study progresses, you may begin to see how the Five Doors can be used in a discussion with your teen, or how it may contribute to your marriage. Don't be afraid to use the concepts in other relationships, considering how you are guarding the doors in that particular relationship. The writer of Proverbs wasn't focusing on any single age group. I believe He was providing a method of looking at and pursuing purity that could help anyone at any age.

The Planned Purity® Blueprint

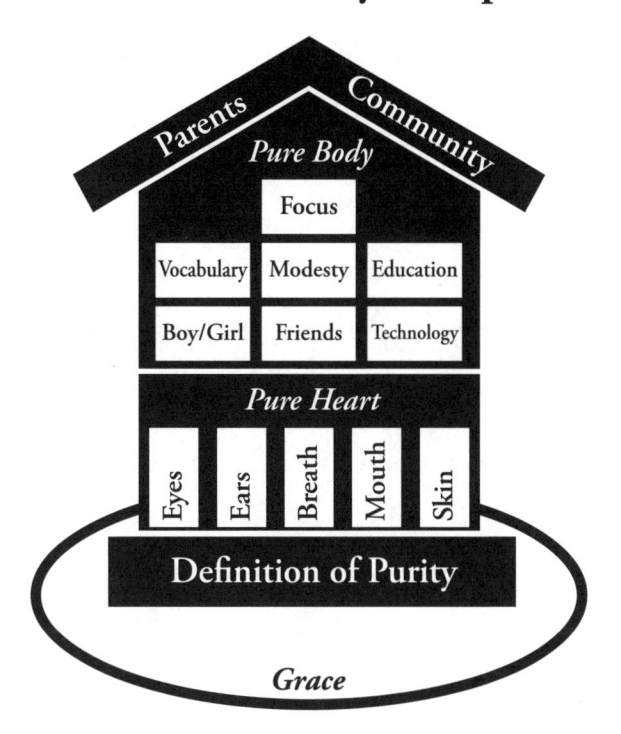

```
                    Parents / Community
                         Pure Body
                           Focus
              Vocabulary  Modesty  Education
              Boy/Girl    Friends  Technology

                         Pure Heart
              Eyes  Ears  Breath  Mouth  Skin

                    Definition of Purity

                            Grace
```

Welcome to this Planned Purity® parent-child study! If you're learning about the Five Doors approach to purity training for the first time, we think you'll be delighted with this small group experience, coupled with lessons for your child from *The Princess and the Kiss* and *The Squire and the Scroll* storybooks. If the Planned Purity® blueprint is already familiar to you, please use this information for review.

As you proceed with this study, you'll see that the weekly readings correspond to the foundation and first floor of the diagram above. The foundation of the house is an accurate definition of purity, which is followed by the first floor, the Five Doors of the Heart (the basis for the story *The Squire and the Scroll*). This five-part maintenance program for a pure heart establishes the groundwork for a complete understanding of sexual purity in the coming years.

The second floor introduces the Seven Windows of Opportunity. These windows help set boundaries for interaction that contribute to sexual purity more specifically.

The roof of the house represents accountability and mentoring. Without others who help us pursue purity, our house is vulnerable to elements that can destroy what's been taught and practiced.

Finally, the house is surrounded by a circle of grace, reminding us that failure and forgiveness are integral to the pursuit of real purity.

In this study we'll be focusing on the foundation, the first floor, and the circle of grace. For a complete explanation of the blueprint and the entire Planned Purity Training System, please visit www.purityworks.org. Many other resources are available for continuing parent and child development after this study. You may want to read *Planned Purity for Parents,* or begin a study with your child using the *Life Lessons* guides based on the *The Princess and the Kiss* and *The Squire and the Scroll* for children 8-12.

How to Use This Book

Following is an explanation of how to use the content of this program for small group study and for instructing your child. Each weekly lesson has an accompanying video by Jennie Bishop to introduce the theme and aid in group discussion.

1. Children's Storybooks

This study for parents is designed to work in tandem with two children's storybooks: *The Princess and the Kiss* and *The Squire and the Scroll*. If you do not already own copies of these, you will find them available for purchase at most Christian bookstores or online at warnerpress.org. Reading these books to your child is recommended as you teach the weekly lessons.

The Princess and the Kiss was written in response to my own daughter's kindergarten declaration, "Mom, all my girlfriends have boyfriends. I need a boyfriend, too." This best-selling picture book about the Princess who saves her "kiss" (portrayed as a ball of light in a bell jar) for a worthy suitor has become a favorite of hundreds of thousands of children around the world.

The Squire and the Scroll followed as a boy's companion to *The Princess and the Kiss* and introduces children to the concept of the Five Doors of the Heart featured in this study. When an evil dragon steals the Lantern of Purest Light from his kingdom, the Squire sets out with the king's last knight to retrieve it. During the adventure, five quests must be completed to overcome the dragon and restore the Light to the people.

2. Weekly Meetings/Chapter Readings

This study may be done in a group or by a parent on his or her own. If meeting as a group, a pastor, teacher, or parent should serve as a facilitator. You can find the Leader's Guide at warnerpress.org.

Each person should read the weekly chapter before attending class and mark passages that are meaningful or evoke questions. Take time to watch and listen for the Holy Spirit's leading, and feel free to steer away from the contents of the book to the questions of the parents in attendance. Be sensitive to God's cues to break away from the "plan" in each gathering.

This said, the group should understand that meetings are not personal counseling sessions. Individuals must agree to keep what is shared in meetings in confidence so that safety and support can be achieved. Respect each other, encourage, but don't try to "fix." Give each other a safe place to wrestle with the application of the material in each family. Start a group Facebook page or group text, if you like, to share your thoughts or personal experiences as you read or interact with your children during the week.

You can sign up for regular emails at the website, www.purityworks.com. You can also see daily posts on purity and related family issues by liking the "PurityWorks with Jennie Bishop" page on Facebook. Questions can always be posted there for community discussion.

At the introductory meeting, every parent will be asked to come prepared for next week by reading the first lesson, following the first week of short devotions, and doing the object lesson that week with your child. If you haven't yet read *The Princess and the Kiss* and *The Squire and the Scroll* with your child, you should also do that as many times as you and your child like. Remember, although *The Princess* seems to be a story for girls, the suitors in the story have a lot to teach young boys. It's helpful for boys to understand how a young woman is different from them and how she chooses a man with specific godly qualities.

3. Parent Daily Devotionals

Part two of this study was created to give each small group member daily encouragement based on a Bible passage. Only five devotions are provided per week to allow grace for other devotions or needs of the day. You may find it helpful to keep this book next to your bed or in any personal place you will return to each day.

One Scripture passage a week is recommended for memorization. Memorizing has been proven to actually deepen your experience and enrich your understanding of the material studied. Cut out the printed scripture found on the *Five Doors of the Heart* activity pages (FREE download at fivedoors. warnerpress.org) and tape it to your refrigerator or bathroom mirror. Write the verse on an index card and place it in a purse or billfold to review when you have a few minutes. Read the passage a few times a day when you see it.

Please take time to meditate on your short devotion instead of rushing through it. Make it a priority to get your "money's worth" from these life-changing purity concepts for you and your family.

4. Weekly Lessons With Your Child

Following each weekly reading in this book is a prepared lesson for you to share with your child. You will need just a few around-the-house items for the object lesson portion. After you have finished the weekly reading, then read the lesson you will give your child, prepare your supplies, and choose a day and time to do it, allowing a half-hour to an hour.

You do not need to follow the script word-for-word, but use your own words to make the point however you like. Allow for interaction and don't be in a hurry. It's all mapped out for you.

Whether or not your child is actually following Christ, you will find great value in teaching him or her these principles. Furthermore, in learning about the five doors of purity, your child likely will be led to the saving grace of Jesus. Remain prayerful, and be prepared to lead your child to Christ.

The *Five Doors of the Heart* activity pages offer simple, fun activities to reinforce each lesson. You can download them for FREE at fivedoors.warnerpress.org. As you work on these together, talk about key points of the lesson and see if your child remembers what was learned. If your child can't remember, share the key points again briefly.

WEEK 1
Purity: Guarding the Five Doors of the Heart

"My son, pay attention to what I say; turn your ear to my words. Do not let them out of your sight, keep them within your heart; for they are life to those who find them and health to one's whole body. ***Above all else, guard your heart, for everything you do flows from it.*** *Keep your mouth free of perversity; keep corrupt talk far from your lips. Let your eyes look straight ahead; fix your gaze directly before you. Give careful thought to the paths for your feet and be steadfast in all your ways. Do not turn to the right or the left; keep your foot from evil."* Proverbs 4:20-27 (NIV, emphasis added)

A Definition of Purity

A pursuit of purity begins with the definition of the word. Unfortunately, most of us associate the word with sexual purity alone—waiting until marriage to have sexual intercourse or to interact sexually. I know I did.

When my daughter came home from kindergarten announcing that she needed a boyfriend, I freaked out to Jesus a little, and then I wrote a book. *The Princess and the Kiss* became a bestseller that led to all the resources we offer now through PurityWorks, including this study. As those resources developed, God made it more and more clear through His Word that purity had much more to do with the heart than the body.

Building on that "body only" foundation will only increase frustration and anxiety in us and our children. Sexual purity is one small part of the whole definition of virtue. Our tendency to focus *only* on sexual purity is part of the reason that more of us aren't *achieving* sexual purity.

More than 80% of our children aren't following through on commitments to sexual purity.[1] 66% of men ages 20-30 report being regular users of pornography.[2] Women are becoming addicted to porn as well.[3] Statistics indicate that 40-50% of marriages aren't lasting until "death do us part."[4]

---

1 http://world.wng.org/2007/08/sex_and_the_evangelical_teen
2 The Culture of Pornography, R. Albert Mohler, Jr., Baptist Press, 28 December 2005
3 http://www.covenanteyes.com/2013/08/30/women-addicted-to-porn-stats
4 www.cdc.gov/nchs/nvss/marriage_divorce_tables.htm

Those scary statistics give us good reason to be concerned. But a wrong definition of purity is part of the reason these issues continue to escalate. A good heart is the first "floor" when constructing a household of purity and virtue (see Planned Purity Diagram, p. 11). And a right definition of purity is our very foundation. Three key concepts in that definition follow:

1. *Purity is a lifestyle of continual "inner housekeeping" that is taught over a lifetime,* beginning with a clean heart and working its way from the mind and thoughts into the life and actions.

2. *Purity is important at all ages.* Too long have we put all our emphasis on training our teens, missing the occasions to teach prerequisite purity of heart material in our children's younger years. Purity applies at every age.

3. *Purity is about much more than sex.* As stated earlier, the heart is the true center for the roots and practice of purity. If our minds and thoughts aren't clean, our bodies won't act that way.

Getting Ahead of the Game

The Princess and the Kiss focuses on saving the kiss, both symbolically and physically, until the appropriate time and situation. *The Squire and the Scroll* focuses on guarding the heart. That's a good start for initial discussions with children about boundaries in relationships. But maybe a more important role of books like *The Princess* and *The Squire* is the way they lead us into a *culture of virtue,* not just a sexual purity club.

Feeling a part of a culture of virtue creates a greater desire to *pursue* sexual purity. This enthusiasm can be built over time in a relaxed way, without talking about sex too early. A child needs to know he's part of a Kingdom community, that his heart is a treasure to God, and that he's able to maintain integrity in the simplest matters.

The good news for parents is that approaching the concept of sexual purity is easier if a framework for basic virtue is already in place. *The Princess* and *The Squire* stories were written to build that kind of prerequisite understanding.

Purity starts with a heart of virtue, which naturally opens the door to the embrace of sexual purity. The pursuit of a virtuous heart can begin at any time; but ideally it starts in the preschool/elementary years and dovetails into training on sexual purity as a child grows. Stories are the perfect means to start a continuing discussion. Just as Jesus used simple parables to teach a crowd of all ages, so we can use stories in our families to feed and nurture virtuous imaginations and hearts.

Keep in mind that a transformative relationship with Jesus is the only way to be saved. Although we will practice the spiritual disciplines of the five doors together, they will not save us. They are simply tools to lead us to the loving Christ who gave us our senses in the first place, and a way to practice loving Him and becoming like Him through acts of obedience in agreement with Scripture and the Holy Spirit.

Young people who find their place in an authentic relationship with Jesus and a culture of virtue are world-changers. They aren't perfect, but they develop into men and women who understand honor and integrity, protect one another, guard their hearts and bodies, and are rooted in a well-rounded understanding of purity.

Introducing the Five Doors
So how do we keep a heart "clean"? None of us will live a perfect life. Everyone stumbles into failure and selfishness in moments of weakness. With an understanding of this need for many new beginnings as we form habits, let's discuss the basics of a pure heart.

Simply put, our heart is equipped with five "doors," referred to in Proverbs 4:20-27 and demonstrated in *The Squire and the Scroll* as well. Our choices in keeping our hearts pure rest upon our decisions to open and close those doors, allowing honorable influences in and keeping dishonorable influences out.

The five doors relate to the five senses that we learned about in our youngest years. The senses are a gift physically in that they allow us to experience the world in all its color and sound, textures, tastes, and aromas. Life would be bland at best without our senses. But each sense also represents a spiritual door of opportunity for our hearts, thoughts, and inner person.

As an example, to physically guard the sense of sight, someone would choose to wear sunglasses on a hot, bright day. But in viewing the **eyes** as a door of the heart, that person would consider his viewing habits in the context of how the things he views form his thought life and character.

We shut the door to what corrupts the heart, and open it to the things that build virtue.

The **ears** can physically be guarded with ear muffs, but as a door to the heart, we consider our listening habits. What music, speakers, conversations, or scripts will elevate and contribute to the development of a pure heart, and what will erode it?

The door of the **breath** is associated with smell, physically. We protect ourselves, if we're wise, by steering clear of dangerous inhalants and keeping plastics bags away from our infants. But as a door of the heart, the breath is our greatest gift of all—life itself. So we choose to honor and respect life in all its forms.

Who would deny that the door of the **mouth** is difficult to manage? We're careful to guard physically what we put into that opening, but maybe we're not as choosy about guarding what comes *out* of it in regard to its function as a door of the heart. As one teaspoon of poison taken into the mouth can destroy the body, so one well-timed word can either disable its recipient for a lifetime or be held forever in the heart as a token of love.

Finally, the door of **touch** plays a vital role in the condition of our hearts. Just as we would guard the hand with an oven mitt when taking a fresh pizza from the oven, we must guard the sense of touch as a door to the heart by refusing to use it selfishly. Each of us chooses to be ennobled by encouraging others with our sense of touch, or to become a user by ignoring others' needs for sacrificial, sincere affection.

These are the five doors of the heart. As we make careful choices to open or close them, we protect the heart from impurity and contamination, and can teach even little ones to do so, preparing them for a lifetime of love, service, and honor.

Questions to Consider and Discuss:

- How have I understood purity as more than a sexual issue? How do I need to adjust my thinking?

- Discuss the dangers of limiting an emphasis on purity—body and heart—to the teen years.

- When I think of purity, do I include the regular celebration of sex in a marriage? Abstinence as a single parent?

- How may my pursuit of virtue or lack thereof affect future generations?

- Discuss this thought-provoking phrase: "Purity is always redemptive." Is it accurate? Share your comments with the group.

CHILD'S LESSON 1
Purity: Guarding the Five Doors of the Heart

(Note: These lessons may be done with a child as young as five or six if you feel he/she understands the concepts.)

Use the following lesson with your child to clarify his/her understanding of a pure heart as we prepare to teach each of these five doors specifically in future lessons.

Supplies:
- A crown or supplies to make two—one for your child and one for you!
- A glass of drinking water
- A quarter cup of dirt
- Cake, cupcake, or treat (Put a frosting or paper crown on it if you can!)
- Lesson 1 downloadable activity page. You will make a heart with five doors that open to reveal the different senses we will be learning about as they relate to purity. You will want to keep the heart you make for use in future lessons. Memory verse cut-out: Proverbs 4:23 (NIV1984). You may also create your own memory card using an index card.

Craft
Buy a simple crown for your child, or make two out of construction paper, foam sheets, or other materials you have at home. Have fun wearing them together as you talk about today's lesson.

Read 1 Peter 2:9 (NIV): *But you are a chosen people, a royal priesthood, a holy nation, God's special possession, that you may declare the praises of him who called you out of darkness into his wonderful light.*

Ask your child if she understands she is part of a royal family. If she says she does, ask her why and explain that we are sons and daughters of the King of kings, and that makes us princes and princesses. Put a crown on and explain that you are one as well.

Book Reviews
1. Read or remind your child of the story of *The Princess and the Kiss*. (Have the book handy to flip through or review the story briefly, focusing on the fact that the final suitor did not choose the Princess because

of her looks alone.) Ask: Why do you think this man chose the Princess? Was it just because of her looks? (No, he saw that her heart was pure and "sparkled like diamonds.") Why did the Princess want to save her kiss? (To keep her heart pure.)

2. Read or remind your child of *The Squire and the Scroll*. Ask: Did the Squire become a knight because he was handsome, rich, or cool? (No, he understood what the scroll said and did what was right.) What was his reward in the end? (A princess for a wife, a happy family.)

Salvation Message/Reminder

Ask your child what he or she has to do to have a "pure heart" that "sparkles." Ask: Does it mean you have to wash your heart with a hose? Are we talking about our physical heart or the special part inside of us that God has given to make us unique from everyone else?

Clearly explain the salvation message—that God sent His Son, Jesus, to die for our sins and that when we ask Him into our hearts, He will make our hearts clean. Take time at the end of this lesson to ask if your child would like to ask Jesus to come into his/her heart. What a great opportunity!

Object Lesson

Pour a glass of water. Have your child take a drink. Now add some dirt to the water. Ask: Why wouldn't we want to drink from the glass now? (germs, sickness)

Explain that this is why a pure heart is important. When we let dirt, or sin (explain sin clearly as wrongdoing or wickedness with brief examples), into our hearts, we get them dirty. Dirty hearts make other people dirty. We aren't acting like royalty anymore. And that's when we need Jesus to forgive us. He died on the cross so we could ask Him to come into our hearts, and He forgives us when we are truly sorry for our sin. When we let Jesus take away our sin, we have clean hearts that will help keep other hearts clean, too!

Scripture Verse

Look up Proverbs 4:23 in your Bible and read it with your child. Make sure he understands what it means. Talk about words like "guard" and "wellspring" and define if needed. Ask: What does it mean to guard our hearts (to keep them clean)? (Put the verse on a bathroom mirror or refrigerator for daily and weekly review. When reciting the verse, have your child point at the heart you made together.)

The Five Doors of the Heart Activity

Work with your child to make the heart from the downloadable activity page for Lesson 1. You will introduce the Five Doors of the Heart using the heart you've made. Start with the eye, ear, nose, mouth, and hand covered by the doors. Only talk about the doors—don't open them yet. Use a nearby door and ask your child if he would open it if a monster were outside. (Have fun! Go outside and roar and make a fuss! He will probably say he won't open the door.) Then ask what your child would do if it were an ice cream cone. (Act it out again. The answer should be that he would open the door.)

Don't go into detail, but review the five senses as you open the doors on the heart, and explain that this heart is a way we remember to keep our real hearts clean after they are safe in Jesus. Let your child know that you will be using your heart project every week and learning more about one of the five doors each time.

These suggestions may help with your brief descriptions:

1. The door of the eyes: open to look at good and helpful things; close to things that are private or impure.

2. The door of the ears: close to bad words in songs, movies, and mouths; open to kind, good words, songs, and shows.

3. The door of the breath: close to acts that hurt others; open to respect and care for all living things.

4. The door of the mouth: open to say words of truth and help; close to stop saying hurtful words or lies.

5. The door of the skin: open to touch that helps; close to touch that hurts.

Snacktime and Prayer

Have cake or a treat! Pray together and thank the Lord that He sent His Son for you and enabled you to be part of His royal family. Pray for a pure heart so you can honor your King every day with the choices you make and the thoughts you think.

Homeplay (Instead of homework!)

Let your child play with the cup and dirt this week as well as the heart you made. Remind him/her of the lesson you shared. Read the storybooks again. Recite the child's Scripture verse together once a day, and then try to say it to each other without looking.

Salvation Opportunity

If your child has not yet made a decision for Christ, ask if he/she would like to. Don't push, just make sure your child understands and is prepared to do so one day. If your child is willing, pray with him to ask Jesus into his heart. This is an awesome opportunity that you can make available or refer to anytime throughout the coming lessons.

1.1 Devotion: Pure Hearts See God

What Is Purity? Memorize Proverbs 4:23 (NIV1984)
Above all else, guard your heart, for it is the wellspring of life.

Blessed are the pure in heart, for they will see God. Matthew 5:8 (NIV)

"I used to think that purity was all about saving sex for marriage—but now I understand that purity is really about being able to see God."

Sexual integrity is almost always our first impression when the word "purity" is spoken, and that's unfortunate. Anxiety is naturally our emotional response to a hyper-sexualized society when our child is involved.

It's time to look at purity in a different way, setting aside the worthy pursuit of chastity for just a moment as we consider a broader view of what God wants for us. In reading Matthew 5:8 above, we find that Jesus makes the reason for purity clear. The reason we should guard the heart above all else and keep it pure is because *God wants us to see Him!*

Seeing God is what transforms us from the inside out. When we keep our hearts clean, we see through the window of our physical world to the other side where God is waiting for us to look. He *wants* us to see Him.

Isn't that reason enough to pursue purity? In securing a glimpse of the God of the universe, won't we be forever changed? Won't we be motivated and empowered for anything when we see the love in His eyes? When we see that He accepts and forgives us, won't we be devoted to Him forever?

God isn't looking to beat us up because we continuously make poor choices. God wants to show us the way to freedom and joy. And the thought of seeing Him should be what motivates us to pursue purity, not a fear of lost physical virginity. *The Princess* is not just a chastity parable, but a story of a heart that longs to be pure.

When we see God's face, all our efforts will be worth it. And any stumbles will be swallowed up by the look in His eyes that says, "I love your heart." Now *that's* a reason to pursue purity.

Are you able to set aside the idea of purity as being related to sex alone? How does the idea of seeing God motivate you so much more in your own life, and in teaching your child? If sexual purity is not the end-all, but rather the natural result of getting a good look at God, how would your focus change?

1.2 Devotion: Above All Else

What Is Purity? Memorize Proverbs 4:23 (NIV1984)
Above all else, guard your heart, for it is the wellspring of life.

The heart is deceitful above all things and beyond cure. Who can understand it?
Jeremiah 17:9 (NIV)

"I'm understanding that I can start training my child in purity of heart before we get into the body stuff. Nobody taught me that when I was growing up, so I might have catching up to do."

God doesn't just ask us to guard our hearts—He asks us to do so *above all else*. Nothing is more important. Why? Our hearts are incredibly vulnerable, and as we'll learn in the next couple of sessions, everything we do springs from our hearts. If we make a pure heart our goal, we can help our children strengthen the foundation for pursuing sexual integrity in the years ahead.

But, just as Proverbs 4:23 brings a sigh of relief for us as a parent, Jeremiah 17:9 should motivate us to examine our own hearts. Have we been deceived in any way? Are we missing the basics of purity? Have we spent most of our time wondering about sex-related issues and forgetting about our basic heart condition? As we consider aspects of purity, we may find that we are missing a little groundwork ourselves.

When we examine the reasons for our choices, we strengthen and purify our hearts and faith so we can accomplish the awesome things God wants to do through us (see 2 Corinthians 13:5). Be willing to replace a few bricks in your own foundation as you teach your child from scratch, so your whole family will pursue purity more successfully.

Our culture is flippant about the guardianship of the heart. But we can't afford to live on cultural autopilot, where we simply adopt the practices of mainstream society. We have a high calling, and we're called to guard the heart *above all else*.

Like the Princess in *The Princess and the Kiss*, we and our children can learn to evaluate choices every day—and not just when potential husbands or wives come calling.

Our own purity is a legacy we leave for our families. How is your heart today?

Examine your heart, for your own sake as well as for your children's sake. Pray for God to open your eyes to any way in which you may have become desensitized or casual about your own pursuit of a pure heart and life. Determine to allow God to change YOU in this study, not just your child.

1.3 Devotion: Absolute Purity

What Is Purity? Memorize Proverbs 4:23 (NIV1984)
Above all else, guard your heart, for it is the wellspring of life.

Treat younger men as brothers, older women as mothers, and younger women as sisters, with absolute purity. 1 Timothy 5:1-2 (NIV)

"How can I be absolutely pure? Everyone is so casual in their interactions, but I want to be above reproach in the way I relate to others, especially the opposite sex, and teach my kids the same standards."

We should treat younger men and women as "brothers and sisters," not "boyfriends and girlfriends"? Yes, we're being called to swim against some strong cultural norms!

"Absolute purity" is a tall order, but also broader than it seems. It includes not only guarding ourselves against inappropriate liaisons, but also showing respect, getting rid of anger or bitterness, being honorable in our speech, and a whole variety of actions that reflect integrity in relationships (see Ephesians 4:31).

God uses strong words to make it clear that impurity is not a practice of His people, but He never meant to limit its pursuit to sexual behavior alone. God calls us to pursue all purity, not just the part that relates to our physical desires.

In *The Princess and the Kiss*, the Princess takes her father seriously when he warns, "Never part with it (the kiss) for the sake of a stranger." She knows that parting with her kiss without thinking could devastate her carefully-guarded heart. We make our choices with prayerful consideration as well. Every experience of life has the potential to contribute to the purity or contamination of our precious hearts.

The call to "absolute purity" reflects how beloved we are to God. He's not trying to spoil our fun; instead, He's trying to give us a key to a treasure. The reward of a wildly blessed life can be found on this course that few choose: the courageous pursuit of purity.

In your interaction with others, how do you treat the opposite sex? Do you practice appropriate boundaries and treat others respectfully, as you would a brother or sister? Your child will learn much about how to interact from your example. Ask the Lord to help you evaluate today any way that you might fine-tune your actions toward others to come closer to God's broader definition of purity.

1.4 Devotion: Inside Out

What Is Purity? Memorize Proverbs 4:23 (NIV1984)
Above all else, guard your heart, for it is the wellspring of life.

Woe to you, teachers of the law and Pharisees, you hypocrites! You clean the outside of the cup and dish, but inside they are full of greed and self-indulgence. Blind Pharisee! First clean the inside of the cup and dish, and then the outside also will be clean. Matthew 23:25-26 (NIV)

"I can be great at looking put together on the outside. I know all the right answers. But now I see that my heart has to be in the right condition to be pure."

This verse provides a helpful picture of what purity from the inside out is all about. The Pharisees could put on a good show, but on the inside, their motivation came from selfishness. While they were parading around in their holy garments, they were seething on the inside with pride and condescension.

No show of religiosity or false goodness can cover an ugly heart (see 1 Samuel 16:7).

Have you ever met someone who wore their distaste for sexuality or immodesty like a "holy garment"? They have used their pious attitude to look down on others. Unfortunately, that appearance of "holiness" is no better than a beautiful woman who uses her looks to take advantage of men, or a handsome man who charms women into foolish choices. In either case, the appearance of the person may appeal in some way, but an impure heart is obviously evident.

God made us for so much more. He gifted us with our bodies and all their complexities. Furthermore, He provided in Jesus a way to develop a heart that would reflect His very nature from the inside out. We're participating in this study to learn how to wear those pure hearts on our sleeves.

Remember Prince Peacock in *The Princess and the Kiss*? What an example of a man absorbed in self-importance and appearances! His muscles commanded attention, but his eyes were on the little mirror, admiring himself. And as Ben Franklin once said, "A man wrapped up in himself makes a very small bundle."

That's why we pursue purity. To escape the "smallness" of the selfish, polluted heart.

Part of parenting toward purity is knowing your child's heart. What heart issues might be contributing to actions that concern you? Pray that God will correct not only actions, but hearts, in both you and your child.

1.5 Devotion: Real Love

What Is Purity? Memorize Proverbs 4:23 (NIV1984)
Above all else, guard your heart, for it is the wellspring of life.

And this is my prayer: that your love may abound more and more in knowledge and depth of insight, so that you may be able to discern what is best and may be pure and blameless until the day of Christ, filled with the fruit of righteousness that comes through Jesus Christ—to the glory and praise of God. Philippians 1:9-11 (NIV)

Week 1: Purity

"When I hear the word love, I most often think about flowers and romance. But now I know that real love is also about protection, integrity, and honoring a beloved."

So many people talk about love as if it is mysterious. It appears, it disappears, and no one can possibly understand it. But God expects us to grow in our knowledge of what love is, to acquire a greater depth of insight. He explains that we'll be able to know what is best and how to be pure and blameless, bearing righteous behavior like fruit on a tree. When we pursue purity, we become experts at real loving.

So is love really so mysterious? Perhaps the feelings connected with romantic love can spin a person around, but true love is so much more than "falling." It is rooted in protection and a willingness to sacrifice for the best of the other person (see 1 Corinthians 13:4-8). It is taught, exemplified, and birthed in a healthy family that loves to the point of sacrificing for each other as Christ did for us.

When a child understands true, sacrificial love, that understanding is much more likely to rule over the "spinning" that so often carries young people into sexual experimentation. True love longs to protect the beloved's wholeness and freedom, not to possess the person. It longs for him or her to have what is best, not what either person simply "wants."

In *The Princess and the Kiss*, the Princess' head certainly could have been turned by muscles, flowers, or beautiful clothes. But she always went back to wondering how the men would value her and her kiss. She knew she was looking for a love that would not only make her heart pound, but would last through all the ordinary days of life.

The Five Doors of the Heart can help prepare each one of us to recognize such love.

To nurture a child who will steer clear of cheap love substitutes, teach true love at home in actions and explanation. As always, the whole family's best example is Jesus. His simple kindness, growing in the heart of a child, is the first step to loving a spouse and family well later on.

WEEK 2
The Door of the Eyes

The first of the Five Doors of the Heart is probably the most powerful influence of all in shaping us. The eyes are the door to nature, television, the faces of our families, movies, computer screens, concerts, and everything else we look at. Assessing these viewing habits can help form and free our hearts to love and value what really matters.

During my childhood years on the farm, I remember my father telling us about a coming solar eclipse. On the day of the event, he took us into the yard and gave each of us a turn looking through his welding mask to see what was happening. We were to look the other way until we had the mask on, to guard our eyes.

This is a perfect example of guarding the physical eyes. We wear sunglasses when the sun is bright, goggles when we're in a dirty working environment, and we steer clear of those pointy objects our moms are always warning us about. But what does it mean to guard the eyes of our hearts?

Most young children know that there are things we should look at and things we shouldn't. But as we age, it's easy to get more lax about these choices. We're grown-ups, after all. We can handle it. But *let him who thinks he stands take heed, lest he fall* (1 Corinthians 10:12, NKJV). Habitual viewing forms us, and can subtly take over our lives.

Viewing habits form our thought life and practices. If they didn't, no company would waste money on advertising. Beer commercials sell beer, and cigarette smokers beget more cigarette smokers. Television programs that feature sexual content (and more than 70% of them do [5]) lead our minds regularly into sexual thoughts, curiosity, and hunger. Pornography, the visual pandemic of our time, destroys with its objectification and highly addictive

---

[5] Dale Kunkel, Keren Eyal, Keli Finnerty, Erica Biely, & Edward Donnerstein, "Sex on TV 4," Kaiser Family Foundation, November 2005, http://www.kff.org/entmedia/upload/Sex-on-TV-4-Full-Report.pdf

qualities. Violence begets violence, as we've seen from the evidence in so many school shootings. These are the eclipses that can blind us to the beauty of truth, nature, good food, self-control, and healthy recreation.

Males are especially affected by visual stimulation, and must learn to set boundaries for online, television, and computer endeavors. Face-to-face relationships are put in jeopardy when onscreen images seem easier to manage. "Bouncing the eyes" away from explicit content, as described by Stephen Arterburn in *Every Man's Battle*, is an excellent habit to develop.[6]

Our children are being formed by what they watch. The screen is not a trustworthy babysitter and needs our management to support a culture of virtue. It's up to us either to evaluate before viewing, or turn it off. A number of online resources exist to help choose movies wisely. Use them yourself, and then teach your child how to use them. Don't allow unsupervised viewing of random material for lengthy periods of time. Know what your family is watching and agree together that you will set no vile thing before your eyes (see Psalm 101:3, NIV).

Don't set these limits because of what *you* think, but because of what *God* thinks. He wants you to enjoy your own life, not to be chained to a virtual existence. How much time is passive viewing stealing from your family? How many video games have kept you from conversations where understanding could take place? How many addictions have begun with an open door to just one more hour of programming?

Always imagine Jesus being physically in the room with you. (He actually is there, you know.) What would He think of your viewing? Would He laugh along with you, or would He have to leave the room? This simple exercise could change many questionable viewing habits. If you don't feel confident enough to have the Lord in on what you're watching, shut the door of the eyes immediately.

All that said, there is plenty to open the eyes to, especially in nature. Getting outside in a society that tends towards a virtual, indoor existence is a major plus. Kids who grow up appreciating the natural world have less tendency to end up screen-locked. They want more than that.

---

6   Arterburn, Stephen, Fred Stoeker, Mike Yorkey. Every Man's Battle: *Every Man's Guide to Winning the War on Sexual Temptation One Victory at a Time*. WaterBrook Press, 2004. Print.

Satisfying the hunger for curiosity and new experiences can always take place with outdoor activities, new hobbies, board games, and other activities that keep us face-to-face. Make a list of many creative and active pursuits for your child to choose or complete before screen time is offered each day.

We can be tech and media savvy while setting boundaries to keep this time suitably corralled. A helpful contract from Planned Purity® for the whole family to use in beginning the discussion is available in the back of this book (see page 91).

Hopefully the concept of the door of the eyes is coming into focus for you now. Some examples of the open-and-close that clarify guarding the heart in this way are below:

- Adults: Open your eyes to the eyes and body of a spouse. Close them to any other tempting substitute.

- Teens: Open your eyes to parents, trustworthy friends, and authorities. Close your eyes to inappropriate posts, apps, and sexual content to protect your heart and future.

- Children: Open your eyes to the wonder of the outdoors. Close your eyes to technology unless Mom and Dad approve.

Questions to Consider and Discuss:

- Read Matthew 6:22-23. What can we say about the importance of intentionality in our choice of content and viewing practices?

- What viewing habits do you practice right now that you know in your heart are questionable?

- What boundaries do you want to set for the child/children in your household? Should they be different than the ones you set for yourself? Why? Be specific.

- What is your greatest concern for your children when it comes to the door of their eyes? Allow other members of the group to share what approaches have been helpful to them in these matters.

CHILD'S LESSON 2
The Door of the Eyes

Supplies:
- Sunglasses, goggles, or protective mask
- A sharp stick or bright light
- Samples of good reading material, movies, or games
- Gumballs or cookies (could be decorated as eyes)
- Lesson 2 downloadable activity page. You will make a face with glasses that can be put on and off as we learn about protecting our eyes to help us keep our hearts pure. Memory verse cut-out: Psalm 101:3 (NIV). You may also create your own memory card using an index card.

Demonstration
Let your child try on the sunglasses, goggles, or mask. Ask: Why do we wear these things? Use the light or stick (carefully) to show how the protection works. (The child should understand what things protect our eyes, what could harm them, and think/talk about how.)

The Five Doors of the Heart Activity
Use the heart you made in Lesson 1 to reintroduce the five doors. (Start with all five doors closed, and open them one by one to review the doors of the heart. Then close all doors except the one covering the eye.) Ask: How do we need to guard our eyes to keep our hearts clean? Give your child time to think. Then add to your child's ideas if he/she needs help.

Work with your child to color and cut out the downloadable activity page for Lesson 2. Ask: How many things can you think of that could hurt our eyes? Have your child put the glasses on the face and talk about how they protect our eyes in each situation. Then take the glasses off again. Repeat as long as your child is interested.

Book Review
Remind your child of the story of *The Squire and the Scroll*. (Have the book handy to flip through or review the story briefly, focusing on the scene in the cave). Ask: How did the Squire use the shield? (To guard his eyes.) What did the knight do? What happened to him? What happens when

we're not careful about what we look at? (Our hearts get dirty. We can be full of fear, feel ashamed, or start to act like the bad things we see.)

Discussion

Ask: What will you do to make good choices about what you look at? (Ask Mom and Dad before viewing, tell Mom and Dad if I see something uncomfortable, close my eyes or turn my head, turn something off.) Have your child name good things to look at. (Good media, animals, birds, plants, people, faces and pictures of family, the Bible and good books, etc.) Give some examples and ask your child to close or open his eyes, according to what he thinks he should do. (Lady in a bikini, a beautiful painting, a bug, a flower, a man shooting people, a picture on someone's phone....) Have fun discussing!

Activity

Find a short, simple, how-to video online and watch it together. (Could be how to fold a napkin, how to tie a knot, etc.) Now, do what was taught. When you're finished, explain how watching the video taught you how to do something fun. Some videos teach you bad habits instead. What we watch makes us want to copy. This is why we need to guard our eyes.

Scripture Verse

Look up Psalm 101:3 (NIV) in your Bible and read it with your child. Define the words "approval" and "vile" together. Put this week's memory verse on the front of your television or computer.

Snacktime and Prayer

Have fun putting gumballs or cookies up to your eyes and taking silly pictures. Pray together and ask the Lord to help you be as brave as the Squire. Pray for the wisdom and courage to close eyes to bad things and open them to good things. Thank God that He is showing your family how to have pure hearts!

Homeplay

Let your child play with the sunglasses, goggles, and mask as well as the Lesson 2 activity you made and remind him of what he learned. Read the storybooks again. Recite the child's Scripture verse together once a day, and then try to say it to each other without looking.

2.1 Devotion: God Sees

The Door of the Eyes: Memorize Psalm 101:3 (NIV)
I will not look with approval on anything that is vile.

For the eyes of the LORD range throughout the earth to strengthen those whose hearts are fully committed to him. 2 Chronicles 16:9 (NIV)

"Sometimes it seems like we can't look anywhere. It's a constant challenge to turn off the TV or look away from life-sized posters at the mall. But our family is counting on God's help, and we're not giving up!"

If we're devoted to guarding our hearts and our families from impurity, 2 Chronicles 16:9 is good news. We may struggle with the door of our eyes, but God's eyes are looking at us! In a world where explicit themes are emblazoned everywhere we look, God is looking for squires with shields up like the young man in the story.

When we discipline ourselves and teach our kids to look away, when we set aside precious time to evaluate what others generally think is "no big deal," God makes it a point to strengthen us. One of His Hebrew names is El Roi, "the God who sees me" (see Genesis 16:13).

In God, who is Light, there is no darkness at all. God wants us to be safe in His holiness. Our destiny is not to be trapped like that proverbial frog in the pot, letting culture wash over us, getting hotter and hotter until we boil in addiction and brokenness. Instead of drowning in foolishness, we can think critically and know our limits.

God loves the "light" in you! Keep evaluating your viewing habits to keep them from contributing to a numb, darkened conscience. Consider a "reset" week off from technology to get a fresh perspective on what is God-honoring and what isn't. Hold up your shield of faith and refuse to let your heart be polluted by questionable images and content. God supports you as you set a valiant example for your family!

Take note this week of images that disturb you. Are there any? If not, you may be numb. Imagine that your child is with you. Do more images bother you now? Why or why not? Make the hard choices to set the example for your child, and remember God will strengthen you.

2.2 Devotion: Deadly Invisibles

The Door of the Eyes: Memorize Psalm 101:3 (NIV)
I will not look with approval on anything that is vile.

I have set the LORD *continually before me; Because He is at my right hand, I will not be shaken.* Psalm 16:8 (NASB)

"Some thoughts and images that cycle through my mind are negative or unhealthy. I'm learning to replace those images with God's Word over and over until I am thinking of Him. That's one way I practice guarding the door of my eyes."

Our thoughts (thank God) are invisible. No one would want his thoughts broadcast on a jumbo screen. Only our personal, spiritual eyes know what is in our heads. And we're the only ones who can correct this internal viewing.

The knight in *The Squire and the Scroll* reveals his thought life when he growls, "I have not become a knight because of any scroll." His proud estimation of himself results in actions that turn him to stone. Guarding our hearts by paying attention to what we imagine in our minds is as important as what we choose to physically look at. Carefully considering what we're thinking about can set us free from the bondage of longstanding lies.

What "wallpaper" lines your mind's eye? Our child's unkindness may be the result of thoughts about being bullied at school. A spouse may be grumpy because he is musing over a debt that threatens the financial security of his family. The cure for our fear-based behavior is to "look" at God or "set Him before us," using His Word to reflect on His great Person and power, instead of our circumstances.

We remind ourselves that we are strong in Jesus: *I can do all things through Christ who strengthens me* (Philippians 4:13, NKJV). We can position ourselves as fearless when we are covered by God's protection: *The* LORD *is the stronghold of my life—of whom shall I be afraid?* (Psalm 27:1, NIV). Peace will flood in and wash away unwelcome thoughts. We guard the heart when we practice filling ourselves with God and His truth instead.

Next time you are anxious, evaluate your thoughts and begin a new habit. What are you seeing in your mind's eye? Replace that thought with an image that relates to a suitable Bible verse to replace the anxiety.

2.3 Devotion: Outward Appearances

The Door of the Eyes: Memorize Psalm 101:3 (NIV)
I will not look with approval on anything that is vile.

I not look with approval on anything that is vile. Psalm 101:3 (NIV)

"Being holy and pure directly relates to what I look at. And what I look at sets the standard for my family. If I want purity for them, I have to set clear boundaries for us all."

"Vile" isn't a word we use much in everyday conversation. It means "worthless" or "wicked." That broad definition can include a lot of what we view as entertainment today.

God isn't against media or entertainment, but He is very specific about having nothing to do with wickedness. So we have to decide if *watching* wickedness means we're having something to do with it. What do you think?

I read a story about a family who taped a note with Psalm 101:3 to the top of their television screen, and how deeply that small act affected their viewing habits. That's the power of the double-edged sword of Scripture. It pierces our heart and motivates us to step back and think twice (see Hebrews 4:12).

In *The Princess and the Kiss*, when the Princess considered her suitors, they looked good on the outside. Prince Peacock had muscles. Prince Romance probably had a perfectly groomed mustache. And Prince Treasurechest was no doubt well dressed. But the Princess could see that their hearts weren't interested in her precious kiss. Appearances can be deceiving.

Today's "great family entertainment" is similar. We may consider the content and decide, "Not *my* family." After all, our family isn't just any family. It's a royal family, a sacred family, and so we don't have to be shy about setting standards to guard the door of the eyes.

What movies or shows have you watched lately that pushed the limits of the biblical boundaries you mean to set for your family or yourself? Did marketing, with its catchy slogans and hooks, coax you to watch? Curiosity is normal, but guardrails are needed. Come up with one new way your family can be more intentional and clear about avoiding pitfalls in modern entertainment.

2.4 Devotion: Fire Prevention

The Door of the Eyes: Memorize Psalm 101:3 (NIV)
I will not look with approval on anything that is vile.

But each one is tempted when, by his own evil desire, he is dragged away and enticed. Then, after desire has conceived, it gives birth to sin; and sin, when it is full-grown, gives birth to death. James 1:14-15 (NIV 1984)

"All I need is one look at inappropriate material to get dragged into a second viewing opportunity. Imagine how vulnerable my kids are! That's why we're stressing boundaries and positive technology use in our home."

This graphic verse reminds us of the subtlety of the thoughts and emotions, which are a fertile breeding ground for the online technology and social media of our modern world. A voiced crush can easily turn into an obsession; angry words can become physical violence; an innocent conversation can stir a predator to action. A wealth of opportunities to be coaxed into sin are available to any reader.

Establishing a "no privacy" rule in your household can help. No communication should take place that could not be comfortably viewed, read, or heard by any member of the family. Privacy is too large a responsibility for your child, and possibly for you. The need to hide reflects a probable "dragging away and enticing."

Though it's easy to buy the latest technology and set it free in your home, without guidelines and careful monitoring it can become a destructive beast, rampaging through your family's innocence and relationships like a bull in a china shop. Know your devices. Know your limits. Know how fast a spark can ignite a forest (see James 3:5), and what boundaries in communication you want your children to practice daily.

Think back to *The Squire and the Scroll* and the Squire's unwillingness to look at the walls of the cave, even in the face of the knight's arrogance. We want our children to display that kind of courage in a digital world.

Today, pray for Jesus Christ to set your home apart and guard each family member from the dangers of technology, so every method of communication can be used to glorify Him. Set some clear boundaries, in writing, and enforce them with loving firmness. It can be hard to swim against the current, but much more devastating to drown in it.

2.5 Devotion: Truth That Transforms

The Door of the Eyes: Memorize Psalm 101:3 (NIV)
I will not look with approval on anything that is vile.

Open my eyes that I may see wonderful things in your law. Psalm 119:18 (NIV)

"Memorizing Bible verses seems old-fashioned to many people, but to our family it's a priority. How can we do what God wants if we don't know what He says?"

In some cultures, even a page of the Bible is priceless. When the Book is outlawed, God-hungry people find ways to get hold of a page at a time to read and memorize. Our culture is blessed with such freedom and affluence that we can choose a Bible in any color and translation we like, but the way our Bible looks can never become more important than its content.

Your family desperately needs your leadership to know and study the Word of God. It's the key to being part of a culture of virtue. Even the youngest child can learn shorter verses, and we adults can learn right along with them. Don't be overwhelmed by how many verses there are—just start with a verse you hear at church or read in your own study. Find one that's meaningful to you, in a translation your children can understand. Have fun choosing verses and stories that are meaningful in your home.

Just as we need food every day, we need spiritual food to keep our hearts healthy. And there's no need to starve—we live in a country where we can eat well! We can allow God's Word to judge the thoughts and attitudes of our hearts daily (see Hebrews 4:12).

God's Word is a lamp for our feet and a light for our path (see Psalm 119:105). Like the Squire on his way to the lantern, we don't want to get lost. We need a scroll to light the way. Let God's Spirit guide you, and He will lead your family into truth that transforms from the inside out!

Say a thankful prayer for the gift of the Bible, and ask God to lead you to the passages that will be special treats for your family. Do everything you can to make Scripture a daily part of your family's life. How can you help each other apply this powerful knowledge throughout each day?

WEEK 3
The Door of the Ears

Never have we had as many listening choices as we do today. Thousands of songs, messages, or videos can be carried in our back pockets, but often these many choices crowd out the voices of our family and friends.

Jesus says over and over, "He who has ears, let him hear." Ears that are open to what God is saying make a choice to shut out other distractions. That's what guarding the door of the ears is about. Good input can build wisdom and character, while irresponsible listening can cut deeply into an otherwise healthy heart.

One infamous day in my teenage life, I brought home an album from a well-known artist (yes, in the days before digital recording). Records had large, bright covers, and this one featured a seductively dressed woman, seen through the front window of a car where a man held money along with his steering wheel. My mother was appalled and asked why I had brought such an album into the house.

"Oh, Mom, it's no big deal," I answered. "I just like the music."

Years later, I still remember the words to those songs and would be glad not to have them in my head. But music is a powerful mnemonic device (NEH-mon-ic: a method of remembering). That's why we set Scripture and biblical concepts or doctrines to music, too. People who haven't spent time specifically memorizing Scripture any other way may know a number of Scripture verses just because they listen to Christian music.

Just as seeing things too much can make us numb to corrupting images, so listening too much can make certain words or messages all too common. For instance, are you shocked when you hear, "Oh, God," as a casual expletive? Biblically such a phrase can be considered an outright curse (see Exodus 20:7), but now we may not even notice it. We need God's help to reintroduce sensitivity to our ears.

Popular music isn't subtle in its lyrical content, and neither are many of the videos that result. At the same time, some lyrics and videos are beautiful—even life-changing—especially in Christian music. Our choices in daily listening will help determine how our beliefs and relationships are formed.

Obvious good and evil are apparent, but more subtle influences deserve evaluation as well. A constant soundtrack of produced music shuts out the sound of a loved one's voice, the ocean is drowned by a blasting radio, the wind in the trees is interrupted by a ringing phone. These sounds are not wrong in themselves, but the relief that comes from distancing ourselves for the purpose of quiet reveals something important.

The value of silence has been lost in the hum of noise that daily surrounds us. Even in our prayer times, we're accosted by the roar, and so it's very easy to give up the practice of talking with and listening to God altogether—except in the very short sound bites we've grown accustomed to. How sad, when this is the very reason God gave us spiritual ears! When the physical ears are drowned in chaos, it can be difficult to tune in to God's voice.

Marinating in 24/7 sound and falling asleep to a television can seem natural, but let's consider what life was like before technological devices became so common. Families were able to enjoy birdsong and friends' conversations on front porches instead of a virtual soundscape alone in headphones. We still can!

Regular days or parts of days without technology can help our families reset to each other and to a more natural, relaxing soundscape. It's not always easy, but it's so beneficial. Families who practice periods without TVs and produced music notice less stress, a rediscovery of conversation, crafts, board games, physical activities, hobbies, and time in the kitchen.

How is your family's life shaped by sound? Are the lyrics of your songs consistent with the values you want to instill? When you listen to a favorite, what effect is it having on you? If we want our children to be honest about their influences, we should set the example.

What kind of messages are we allowing in our homes through the story lines of movies and television? How often have we enjoyed natural sounds without anything produced? Are we trying to drown out anxious thoughts? If so, we might be adding even more stress in the process.

Consider what your family could have more of if there were less noise. Would there be less stress? Fewer arguments? Clearer understanding? How would your spouse or family feel if you closed the laptop, turned away from the computer, or put your phone away anytime they approached you face-to-face? What difference would turning the TV off before bed make in your communication or your sex life? Your prayer life?

God created some pretty awesome soundscapes before technology appeared on the scene. Let's crowd out sorry substitutes to make room for what builds pure hearts and a culture of virtue. He who has ears, let him hear.

Questions to Consider and Discuss:

- What music would you like your child to be listening to, ideally?
- Do you regularly evaluate your own listening habits?
- What value do you see in the practice of silence? How about regular "technology fasts" (giving up devices for a regular, set period of time)?
- Research shows that televisions are not good bedfellows. Could your family remove any bedroom TVs and adjust to quiet, or instrumental music? Why or why not?
- What listening habits distract you from God or your spouse/family on a daily basis?
- If your life were a song, which one would you like it to be?

CHILD'S LESSON 3
The Door of the Ears

Supplies:
- Earplugs or cotton balls
- A cotton swab and/or pencil
- Samples of good listening material
- Carrots, celery, or other crunchy, noisy snacks
- Lesson 3 downloadable activity page. You will make a head with earmuffs that can be put on and off as we learn about protecting our ears to help us keep our hearts pure. Memory verse cut-out: Proverbs 19:20 (NIV1984). You may also create your own memory card using an index card.

Demonstration
Let your child try the earplugs, or put cotton in his/her ears. Ask: Why would people wear these? Use the cotton swab or pencil (carefully) to show how the protection works. (The child should understand the concept of protecting our eardrums/hearing.)

The Five Doors of the Heart Activity
Every time the Squire referred to his scroll, he was listening to God's voice. The wool, the shield, the flask, the boots, and the flower were provided at the right times as he listened and looked. God will give us the same attention and guidance as we learn to be aware.

Use the heart you made in Lesson 1 to reintroduce the five doors. (Start with all five doors closed, and open them one by one to review the doors of the heart. Then close all doors except the one covering the ear.) Ask: How can you guard your ears to keep your heart clean? Give your child time to think. Then add to your child's ideas if he/she needs help.

Work with your child to color and cut out the downloadable activity page for Lesson 3. Ask: How many things can you think of that could hurt our ears? Have your child put the earmuffs on the head and talk about how they protect our ears in each situation. Then take the earmuffs off again. Repeat as long as your child is interested.

Week 3: Ears

Book Review
Remind your child of the story of *The Squire and the Scroll*. (Have the book handy to flip through or review the story briefly, focusing on the scene in the woods.) Ask: How did the Squire use the wool? (To guard his ears.) How did that help? (It kept voices out that scared him.) What happens when we're not careful about what we listen to? (Our hearts get dirty. We can be fearful, feel ashamed, or start to do the wrong things we hear about.)

Discussion
Ask: What will you do to make good choices about what you listen to? (Ask Mom and Dad before listening, tell Mom and Dad if I hear something uncomfortable, walk away, turn something off.) Have your child name good things to listen to. (Good songs or musicians, birds, rain, people they love, Bible verses, teachers, etc.) Ask: When is it better to cover your ears? (Loud machinery, music lyrics that sound bad or music that is too loud, cursing and stories that have to be secrets….) Have fun discussing!

Activity
Listen to a favorite song together that is upbeat and encouraging. Talk about how it makes you feel. Ask: What do we do if the music makes us happy, but the words are bad? (Because of the words, choose to protect your heart.) Look at the words to some of your favorite songs and talk about how the words are good (or not). Make hard choices if you discover anything out of line. (This exercise is a great one to do every six months or so.) Be proud and encourage one another to make listening choices that guard the heart.

Scripture Verse
Look up Proverbs 19:20 in your Bible and read it with your child. Talk about what it means to "accept discipline." Clarify who good advice can come from. (We don't want advice from just anyone, i.e. Google is not the best place to look for biblical advice.) What does it mean to be wise? (Not just intelligent, but using knowledge in a way that pleases God.) Put the memory verse where everyone can see it, or in the car next to the radio.

Snacktime and Prayer
Have a snack that is crunchy and noisy. Have fun crunching loudly. Ask: Would the snack be as much fun if it didn't make any sound? Does the crunch make it taste better? What other kinds of food are noisy? (Bubble

gum might be one.) Pray to be a good listener and respect others with good manners. Ask: Now, can you eat a carrot (name the snack you chose) quietly?

Homeplay

Let your child play with the head and earmuffs project you made this week, and remind him/her of what you learned. Reinforce the need to evaluate lyrics. Read the storybooks again. Recite the child's Scripture verse together once a day, and then try to say it to each other without looking.

3.1 Devotion: Music to the Ears

The Door of the Ears: Memorize Proverbs 19:20 (NIV1984)
Listen to advice and accept instruction, and in the end you will be wise.

Whoever has ears, let them hear. Matthew 13:9

"My children notice what I'm listening to, even if I'm not paying attention. I'm making different choices about what we play around the house for the sake of their hearts, but it affects me positively, too!"

Because of the constant stream of sound around us, we tend to tune it out, only taking notice when something major stands out (for parents, this usually includes words like "blood" and "fire"). This can be dangerous when it comes to popular song lyrics. Guarding the door of the ears requires us to tune in when it comes to lyrics. Our children connect deeply with these words that can turn a pure heart into a garbage can.

When we make the effort to listen intentionally as Jesus asks us to do in Matthew 13:9, we can start to take advantage of this amazing memory device to root deep truths in our hearts instead of lies. Setting Scripture and praise to music yields powerful effects against sin (see Psalm 119:11). Positive messages coat our brains with a protective covering that can reject negative messages more readily.

In a world where "me-ism," anger, violence, shocking news, and explicit messages abound, learning to evaluate listening material is a guard against fear and worry as well as against sexual information overload. If we have ears, it's our business not just to "hear," but to hear *wisely.*

When the Squire chooses to plug his ears in *The Squire and the Scroll*, he's learning to keep out fear and stay focused on the road ahead. When the Princess in *The Princess and the Kiss* listens to her parents' advice to save her kiss, it affects the rest of her life. We're giving an irreplaceable gift to our families when we help them learn to open their ears to wisdom and shut them to lies!

Evaluating songs critically and establishing specific family standards in this area sets us apart. Take the time to decide what is allowed in your home, and explain to your family the power of repeated lyrics as they form our thoughts, beliefs, and actions. Let the music in your home strengthen pure hearts!

3.2 Devotion: Sermon Stillness

The Door of the Ears: Memorize Proverbs 19:20 (NIV 1984)
Listen to advice and accept instruction, and in the end you will be wise.

Faith comes from hearing the message, and the message is heard through the words about Christ. Romans 10:17 (NIV)

> *"I've heard some awful words and messages from modern media. If we can get the good stuff into our heads, maybe there will be less room for the junk."*

If faith comes from hearing, then obviously we need to listen to quality content. In a society where everything is shared in short segments, we don't have many opportunities to develop the patience to sit still and ingest a forty-minute sermon. But that doesn't mean we should quit going to church (see Hebrews 10:25). We need that community of faith to feed our hearts and help us stay strong.

Being part of a listening audience is a great way to learn patience. A younger child will probably be wiggly and need drawing paper or a book, but over time he will learn that everyone sits and pays attention. As he grows, he may be able to take some simple notes or draw pictures related to the message. Your discussion before and after also draws him in.

The pastor can deliver information, but it's up to us to use it. On the way to Sunday events, pray together as a family for help in listening and learning. Afterward, in the car or at lunch, discuss what you learned with simple comments on a main point that the whole family can grasp.

The Squire's parents had him memorizing the scroll from a young age, and it brought him a great reward—one that no other knight was able to achieve. That's exactly what a growing knowledge of God's Word will do for our children and families. It's worth every ounce of effort you give to make this active listening and learning a part of family life.

Don't let church attendance become just "that thing that we do." Much valuable information comes from belonging to a church family. Your pastors and children are counting on you to take the lead as a parent. Do your best to use family time in church services as an active listening and learning opportunity.

3.3 Devotion: Hearing God's Voice

The Door of the Ears: Memorize Proverbs 19:20 (NIV1984)
Listen to advice and accept instruction, and in the end you will be wise.

My sheep listen to my voice; I know them, and they follow me. John 10:27 (NIV)

"Hearing God's voice is a kind of listening I want our whole family to develop, but I'm still learning myself. Practice makes perfect!"

The first time a new person calls on the phone, we may ask, "Who is it?" After a few calls, we recognize the voice because we've heard it before. Getting to know God and to hear His voice is a similar process. Isn't it worth it to guard the door of the ears from distractions just to "hear" and "see" God with a pure heart (see Matthew 5:8)?

"Hearing" God's voice doesn't always mean we sense something audibly, although we may. God "speaks" to us through His Word, and sometimes through the words of another person. We may feel His gentle direction as we are praying quietly or pouring out our hearts. During a movie, a "light bulb" may come on. We could experience a deep "knowing" of supernatural guidance or insight, or sense God's touch in our mind's eye or a dream. All of these are ways to "hear" and "see" God.

Staying attuned to God's voice can make all the difference in our attitudes and lives. In *The Squire and the Scroll*, when the Squire listened for God's direction at the pond, his attention made the difference between life and death. As we choose to look for God's insight, He will be faithful to guide us on right paths to purity.

Are you and your family aware that God is with you at all times (see Matthew 28:20)? A constant awareness of His presence makes us ready to hear from Him and respond as Samuel did when he said, *Speak, for your servant is listening* (1 Samuel 3:10, NIV). You can be like Eli and remind your family to be ready!

In your own prayer life, do you allow time for God to respond, or just talk yourself? Discuss with your family God's desire to "speak" and our need to "hear." Practice looking for and pointing out ways each member of your family senses God's leading and voice.

3.4 Devotion: No Storm Too Big

The Door of the Ears: Memorize Proverbs 19:20 (NIV1984)
Listen to advice and accept instruction, and in the end you will be wise.

And this is the confidence that we have toward him, that if we ask anything according to his will he hears us. 1 John 5:14 (ESV)

"Knowing God is listening and wants us to ask for help is so comforting. He wants us to ask for help in parenting. He wants us to ask for help to pursue purity. He hears, and He answers."

During hard times, we may question whether God is listening or even if He is good. But when we look to the Scriptures for answers, we can know for sure that He cares and wants to hear from us. Evil is loose in this world, and there are casualties daily, but we don't have to face those storms alone.

When a thunderstorm strikes, it blots out every other sound with its rumbles. And in the storms of our lives, especially where purity is concerned, the circumstances of our situation can seem very loud and intimidating. But God is bigger, and when we determine to fix our eyes on Him and listen for His voice, we can be at peace. It isn't easy, but it works. He keeps our minds calm when we refuse to listen to anything but Him (see Isaiah 26:3).

Listening only to God is an act of the will that involves a determined replacing of lies with truth. If we choose to listen to the lies in our heads, we will despair, but if we study the Word of God and "listen" to it when we speak and remember it, we will live in hope!

In *The Princess and the Kiss*, when the Princess put her trust in God to bring the right man or no man at all, she relaxed and her heart was at peace. She was listening for His direction and leading. We can do exactly the same. Our hearts can be at rest when we have God's voice in our ears.

Are present circumstances causing turmoil in your family? How can you work together to focus on how big God is instead of the size of the problem? Turn to prayer or certain Bible verses to find strength and peace. God will meet you in the storm.

3.5 Devotion: The Gift of Listening

The Door of the Ears: Memorize Proverbs 19:20 (NIV1984)
Listen to advice and accept instruction, and in the end you will be wise.

My dear brothers and sisters, take note of this: Everyone should be quick to listen, slow to speak and slow to become angry. James 1:19 (NIV)

"We are too busy. I'd like to see our family take more time for listening and less time for running. We need God's help to become intentional in setting aside other things to show love by listening to each other."

Listening is a gift of love to those with troubled hearts, especially when we practice enough self-control to say little or nothing. A hug can be enough after a period of sharing, and very welcome to someone who just needs time and attention.

Fixing things is not what most people need; they need to be heard. Your spouse needs to be heard. Your child needs to be heard. You need to be heard.

Assess how much time your family spends in running from place to place. Does this prevent you from life-changing listening? Do conflicts grow because no time has been spent in listening? Family stress can lessen surprisingly through the simple act of looking into someone's face while she shares her heart.

Think about the way the Princess' fears left when her mother listened. Do you want your family to know that time with you will result in the same peace and freedom from fear? Then listen. Listen hard, long, carefully, and regularly. Evaluate your tendency to get angry or try to fix everything. Stop. Listen.

Where are the best pockets of time for listening in your family life? (i.e., after school in the car, before bed, at the dinner table, etc.) Take advantage of them with full concentration, and then find new pockets where listening can be practiced more often. Watch what happens!

WEEK 4
The Door of the Breath

What are your favorite smells? Fresh chocolate chip cookies? Rain? Flowers? A certain perfume or cologne? Our retail stores are inundated with candles, air fresheners, and all kinds of interesting smells. Some of those smells are said to improve moods, help us sleep, and contribute to our health.

Still, I wear a mask over my nose when I mow the lawn. Otherwise, I puff up like a balloon, my throat tightens, and I collapse into fits of sneezing. I guard my breath physically if I want to finish the job. On a more serious level, we all avoid dangerous inhalants, drugs and cigarettes, or smoke.

Spiritually, guarding the door of the breath is about even more than the gift of smell. We dive deeper to the fact that we have the very breath of God in our lungs (see Genesis 2:7, Job 27:3), and seek to protect and hold all life sacred. We open the door to loving as Jesus did; we close the door to existing for our selfish pleasure. There is no other door like this door; physically or spiritually, there is no life without it.

We start with recognizing how we are loved. God, the Source of life, allows us to live. Through Jesus, we receive spiritual life, too. We have a reason to celebrate and worship with our breath! But not everyone chooses this.

For example, an elderly woman I know grew lonely in her older years and started to drink. Soon, she was a recluse, not relating to anyone. She wasted away in a nursing home although very little was wrong with her physically. Not valuing her life and breath resulted in a sad, lonely end.

But compare her to my neighbor, a young mother who awoke from a difficult birth to find herself an amputee due to a fast-spreading bacteria. Claudia lost both her arms and legs at the elbows and knees, but I never heard her complain. She always talked about how much she could still do, and she set out and did it! That is a door of the breath that is wide open to thanksgiving and hope, guarding the heart against despair.

When we open the door of the breath to thankfulness for our own lives, we come to value others' lives as well. As babies move towards taking their first breath of air outside the womb, we protect them. As romantic relationships come into play, we protect futures by practicing self-control. As an elderly person moves towards taking his last breath, we respect him. As a disabled person gives the gift of her sacred presence, we honor her. When we meet someone from a new culture or ethnicity, we respect differences.

Consider how to cultivate this honor and respect in your household. Make room every day for small kindnesses—compliment check-out people, pay for the person behind you, smile and say hello, take time to learn about a new culture. Teach your children how to love well while guarding against strangers when they are on their own.

Our breath gives opportunity for Jesus' love to come to life in us. There is no other act of obedience as basic as the call to love. Small acts of presence, kindness, a touch, or a smile bring love, honor, and respect with effects deeper than we know.

Guarding the door of the breath may sound sweet and tender, but it also takes incredible courage and faith. This discipline includes shocking concepts like forgiveness and loving one's enemies. Philippians 4:13 tells us that all is possible with God, and when we return unkindness or evil with kindness and good, we evidence Christ's love in a way that is transformational. No one can miss who Christ is when we act in such a way.

We enjoy freedom as we learn to live carefree, but not carelessly. We notice others; they notice us. We respect each other, living things, and our living environments. We make time and room for those who need help.

Whether your child is watering a plant, feeding the dog, praying for a bully, practicing sexual integrity, or standing up for a friend, draw his/her attention to guarding the door of the breath. This fragile, divine gift of life deserves all the support we can offer.

Questions to Consider and Discuss:

- How would you like others to treat you when you are elderly?

- What will happen if your child becomes a parent before marriage? How will that new baby's life be honored? How would you honor and care for your child as a parent in spite of moral failure?

- How do you think a disabled person contributes to the world and to a church family? What would we miss if that person weren't there?

- Does your family recycle or take care of waste responsibly, and see littering as disrespectful to God? How might this affect others and your testimony to them?

- Have you done any kind of mission work in another culture or community? If you have, how did it affect you? If not, why not?

CHILD'S LESSON 4
The Door of the Breath

Supplies:
- An allergy mask (available in drugstores)
- A cigarette and/or other dangerous inhalant like ammonia
- A flower-scented candle or essential oil (item with aroma)
- A potted plant and a pet, if available
- Cookie dough, either homemade or store-bought
- Lesson 4 downloadable activity page. You will make a flower pot with a flower that can be put in and out as we learn about protecting the breath to help us keep our hearts pure. Memory verse cut-out: Job 12:10 (NIV). You may also create your own memory card using an index card.

Demonstration
Let everyone try on the allergy mask as you explain our need to protect ourselves from germs. Talk about which things on the table are good to breathe and which aren't, and why. (Answer curious questions in the case of the cigarette and also make it very clear that cigarettes kill in a very painful way.) Then breathe without the mask. Ask: Do you know that you are breathing the breath of God? Let that sink in. Ask: Can you live without breath? Talk about how amazing it is that God lets us use His breath so we can be alive!

The Five Doors of the Heart Activity
Use the heart you made in Lesson 1 to reintroduce the five doors. (Start with all five doors closed, and open them one by one to review the doors of the heart. Then close all doors except the one covering the nose.) Ask: How can you guard your breath to keep your heart clean? (Help your child out with clues about guarding life and staying safe, helping others, etc. Explain that we will answer that question in today's lesson.)

Work with your child to color and cut out the downloadable activity page for Lesson 4. Have the child smell the flower. Ask: What does the flower smell like? Now, spritz the flower with perfume or cologne. Ask: How does the flower smell now? What would happen if someone sprayed the flower with weed killer? Would we want to smell it then? Why not? Talk with your child about how important it is to be careful of what we breathe in because our life is a precious gift from God.

Book Review
Show your child the page in *The Squire and the Scroll* where the Squire picks the flower and inhales. Ask: Why was the flower so important? (It kept the Squire alive and safe from the poisoned air.) How do plants help us in real life? (They provide oxygen, food, beauty, etc.)

Discussion
Ask: What does God give us when we breathe? (Life.) If God gives you an amazing gift, how must He feel about you? (He loves you.) If God gives others breath, how does He feel about them? (He loves them, too.) If God loves them, should we love them, too? (Yes!) What can we do to love others? (Get creative with exciting acts of kindness—send donuts to a teacher, leave money for the people behind you in a fast-food line or at a toll booth, take a flower to a cashier. Then schedule time as a family to do it!) How can we take care of our animals? They have breath, too. (Take them for walks, feed them, take them out to use the bathroom, brush, pet, etc.) How can we take care of the world God gave us to live in? (Plant care, recycling, not littering, drive less—whatever applies best to your family.)

Activity
Have a real potted plant ready and talk about what someone must do to care for it. If you have a pet, talk about how a pet is cared for. Then talk about how you care for a baby, a grown up, and an elderly person. All these living things deserve our respect, but people are always most important. Why? (Made in the image of God.)

Scripture Verse
Look up Job 12:10 in your Bible and read it with your child. Make sure he/she understands what it means. Talk about the fact that God knows the right time for everyone to live and die, and that we can trust Him even when we feel sad because someone has left us. Life is a very special gift.

Snacktime and Prayer
Have a roll of cookie dough ready so you can quickly enjoy the smell and taste of warm cookies. Thank God for the door of the breath and our sense of smell.

Homeplay

Let your child play with the the mask and the flower pot activity you made this week, and remind him/her of the lesson you shared. Remind your child that God wants us to care for every living thing, especially people. Remind him/her to open this door of the heart to others who breathe, and to close it to hurtful actions, violence, or unkindness. Read the storybooks again. Recite the child's Scripture verse together once a day, and then try to say it to each other without looking.

4.1 Devotion: God's Breath

The Door of the Breath: Memorize Job 12:10 (NIV)
In his hand is the life of every creature and the breath of all mankind.

The LORD God formed a man from the dust of the ground and breathed into his nostrils the breath of life, and the man became a living being.
Genesis 2:7 (NIV)

"I've never realized how much we take life for granted. We are breathing the very breath of God. I'd like us to be grateful every day just to be alive."

Do you remember the day your child took his or her first breath? What a magnificent moment! No one can put breath into a body but God. He's the One who made plants and photosynthesis, crazy kinds of animals, and an incredibly diverse variety of humans.

In our sinful natures, we tend towards ingratitude. We start to complain and see only the problems in our lives. That wrong perspective shuts life off and out. Plants are only weeds. Animals are only pests. And human beings? Well, they're really a pain, especially if you work in customer service!

Our attitude of gratitude (or lack thereof) reveals how we are guarding the door of the breath. A good heart welcomes life and cares for it. A less-than-pure heart tends to forget that simply breathing is a privilege, and finds things to whine about, losing its ability to make a positive impact (see Philippians 2:14-15).

After the return of the lantern in *The Squire and the Scroll*, a group is formed that mentors boys and teaches them to be knights. The men of the kingdom decide to take time and open the door of their breath to these young men to teach them to honor and protect others.

Take a deep breath. Remind yourself that you're breathing the breath of God. He didn't breathe into the animals—He breathed into us. He breathed into you and each member of your family. In His great love, He honors us with this most amazing gift and calls us to serve and protect all that live.

Be grateful for your own life and breath today. How can that God-breath in you connect with the God-breath in others? Perform a random act of kindness for a stranger or two today, as if you are a part of the same family.

4.2 Devotion: Everything That Has Breath

The Door of the Breath: Memorize Job 12:10 (NIV)
In his hand is the life of every creature and the breath of all mankind.

Let everything that has breath praise the LORD. Praise the LORD.
Psalm 150:6 (NIV)

"Life can move so fast with planned events that we forget to appreciate God's creation. He made everything around us for our enjoyment. I'd like to see our family less distracted by extra activities and more content—even delighted—with the world God made."

When our children are small, it's vital that we connect them to the beauty of a flower or the delight of a baby animal. Children who do not notice sunsets and clouds may not notice God Himself as easily. As the heavens declare His glory (see Psalm 19:1), the natural world can easily lead us into an awareness of God and into worship.

God has given us millions of creatures to observe and enjoy no matter where we are. The care and appreciation of bugs, pets, birds, or other wildlife help develop a child's belief in the sanctity of human life as well. If a kitten's life deserves our care and respect, how much more a human being? If litter, waste, and disrespect for the environment are not offenses, what does this say about our respect for the life that is in residence there?

God's created world should never become just a backdrop for our days. It is what He created as a gift to us. Guard against being trapped in a virtual existence away from real people, living things, and the outdoors. This is not the same as real life.

Real life includes important conversations like the one the Princess and her mother enjoyed under the stars one night in *The Princess and the Kiss*. This perfect, natural setting reminded them both of God's immensity and beauty. The heavens made it clear that the God who created a sky full of stars could surely be trusted with the details of a single human life.

Don't make a habit of breathing "canned air" by tuning out of the world around you. Engage with others. Limit screen time. Get outside. Enjoy what God made and spend time caring for it and protecting it. Amazing shifts can result that will close the door of the breath to a toxic, cocooned existence and open it to a life of abundance that God planned for all of us!

How long has it been since you and your family enjoyed a walk, a bike ride, a day at the beach, a snowball fight? Plan for a foray into the natural world once a week, even for a short while. Take time to enjoy animals, pets, and the natural environment. In doing so, enjoy each other and God.

4.3 Devotion: Something Smells Good

The Door of the Breath: Memorize Job 12:10 (NIV)
In his hand is the life of every creature and the breath of all mankind.

For we are a fragrance of Christ to God among those who are being saved and among those who are perishing. 2 Corinthians 2:15 (NASB)

"When I think of our family's lives as an offering to God, I get a whole new perspective. I want God to be pleased with the way we use the breath He gives us, but some days I have to admit that we stink! We need His help to be the fragrant aroma the Bible talks about."

How does your life "smell" to others?

When someone is baking chocolate chip cookies, everyone in the house is led to the kitchen. The aroma and hope of a warm cookie from the oven seem to make everyone happy!

Our lives can be the same to others. As we pursue God's peace and harmony in our homes, others who are hungry for such love and contentment will follow us as though they smell baked goods about to be served!

In the Old Testament a number of passages talk about burnt offerings that were a soothing aroma to God (see Genesis 8:21, Levitivus 2:2). We don't burn things for God since the sacrifice of Christ, but our very lives are now an offering to Him, and we want to smell good!

In *The Squire and the Scroll*, do you remember when the Squire plucked the flower to smell it instead of the toxic fumes in the mountain? Your family can be that flower of safety to someone else, leading that person out of a toxic life into a place of peace and rest. As people watch your family living God's way, valuing the breath of life, they can realize their own value as you welcome them to be a part.

Let's live in such a way that people are drawn to us. That doesn't mean we have to be perfect. It does mean that we model grace, forgiveness, and simple joy in our everyday lives as we seek to be a sweet fragrance to God.

How do you smell? Tell your family about being an offering to Christ, and discuss together when you smell good or bad. Enjoy a discussion with laughter and deeper insights!

4.4 Devotion: A "To-Love" List

The Door of the Breath: Memorize Job 12:10 (NIV)
In his hand is the life of every creature and the breath of all mankind.

And he is not served by human hands, as if he needed anything. Rather, he himself gives everyone life and breath and everything else. Acts 17:25 (NIV)

"Sometimes I act as though God is writing me a report card. But if He gave me breath and died for me, I can relax and just respond to His love by loving others. Why is that such a hard thing to do?"

We can't do anything for God but breathe. He is delighted that we are alive. He has already died for us and taken care of our future. No task we perform can make us loved more or less. We have right standing because of what He did on the cross, but somehow we're still lured back to a spiritual "to-do" list that we think may earn more of God's favor.

God loves you because He loves you, and because love is who He is. God is love (see 1 John 4:8). We are His beloved. Guarding the door of the breath indicates a foundational understanding of this truth: People are loved as they are, completely, by the God who made them. No other person's opinion can change that.

If you're trying to earn God's favor, you may struggle with loving or forgiving in your relationships or in parenting. We can't give what we haven't experienced ourselves. We desperately need to know we are loved and completely forgiven. There is no condemnation for us if we've given our lives to Jesus (see Romans 8:1).

Out of that knowledge, we find ourselves able to love and forgive freely. The Squire in the story showed respect and forgiveness to the knight who failed. He loved him in spite of what he did. The Squire's parents helped cultivate this strong capacity to forgive in their son as they nurtured him with love.

If we have trouble forgiving someone, it may be because we understand love as something to be earned. Let's examine our hearts and open the door of the breath wide to God, who gave the gift in the first place. He is there with open arms to remind us that His love is freely given and that He forgives our sin. Let's toss out that old "to-do" list, and replace it with a "to-love" list instead!

Is there anything you cannot forgive yourself for? Seek the Lord on the matter now to become convinced that He loves you and has forgiven you. You must know you are loved to teach your family the same truth.

4.5 Devotion: Dry Bones Live!

The Door of the Breath: Memorize Job 12:10 (NIV)
In his hand is the life of every creature and the breath of all mankind.

This is what the Sovereign LORD says to these bones: I will make breath enter you, and you will come to life. Ezekiel 37:5 (NIV)

"Not everyone in our family follows God. It's good to know that He is all-powerful and loves our families even more than we do."

Very few perfect "church families" exist. Almost all of us have difficult issues to face, and "dry bones" in our closets! We don't have to be ashamed of this. We live in a fallen world where each one of us is in great need of God.

Plants get diseases. Kittens get distemper. And people die of illnesses physical and spiritual. What can we do when someone we love shows a lack of interest in God, perhaps walking away from Him completely?

The door of the breath opens itself to love in spite of actions, remember? No matter how devastating a loved one's wanderings are, we can care for that person just the same, to the extent he or she will allow. And where that person won't allow, God will pick up the slack.

Why is it that we can show sympathy towards a young unwed mother in a pregnancy center, but fly off the handle if that young woman is our own daughter? We all make mistakes. Our emotions may rise into our throats and overtake us sometimes when our children stumble. Yet, as Isaiah 53:6 says, *We all, like sheep, have gone astray* (NIV).

Most of us are going to face heartache at some point, or disappointment that spins our head around. When that happens, forgive as easily as the Squire forgave the knight. Step in to help and to honor, not to shame. Let God in His omnipotence bring the dry bones to life.

How would you face a great disappointment when it comes to your children or spouse? Ask God to save you from an attitude of judgment, replacing it with the grace to treat such a situation as an opportunity for God to show His power and love.

WEEK 5
The Door of the Mouth

Let's imagine a table spread with mouth-watering food. Right in the middle of that food is a bottle of clearly-marked bleach. Those of us who could read would have no trouble recognizing that the bleach was dangerous poison. It ought to be removed from the other food on the table.

If only we could choose our words as carefully as we choose our food. It isn't what we eat that defiles us, but what we speak that makes our hearts dirty (see Matthew 15:11). And some words are just as poisonous to us and others as that bottle of bleach.

We might use a mouthguard to keep our teeth safe when we're involved in sports, but we need another kind of tool to prevent our mouths from polluting our hearts. We need our tightly-closed lips and the nurturing wisdom of God's Word.

Remember my story about the classmate who called me odd? That word was a bullet that lodged in my heart. It killed any hope of me being "normal" in my small-town community. But my mother helped make up for that.

My mom had a few phrases that I remember well, including her hilarious expression, "Golly Ned!" But the one that affected me most was this: "You can do anything you set your mind to." I've nearly worked myself to death on a few occasions to bring something into being, but, golly Ned, I got it done! Mom said I could, and I believed her. Her words "created" incredible determination in my heart.

There's no denying the importance of guarding the mouth when we read that the tongue is filled with deadly poison (see James 3:8). We can pour out words of "bleach" that destroy a person's self-worth for a lifetime, or words of spiritual nurture that nourish and build up every time they're remembered.

Vulgarity has become commonplace, but it can't be the practice of those promoting a culture of virtue. The world has enough air pollution; it doesn't need any assistance with the words we speak. Cleaner speech results in cleaner thinking, less complaining, and fewer arguments. Vulgar speech degrades a culture. Sexual innuendo goes directly against any pursuit of purity. Using God's name casually has no place in our lives according to the commandments (see Exodus. 20:7).

Marriage experts recommend "zipping the lips" as one of the most important ways to maintain strong relationships. This advice echoes the biblical passage to be slow to speak and quick to listen (see James 1:19). Silence definitely has its place, and this self-control benefits us and our children over and over again.

Dietrich Bonhoeffer, the theologian, was constantly taught by his father to be accurate in his speech. The children of his family were challenged again and again to think about what they said and to speak in such a way that what they voiced was absolutely articulate and true. Bonhoeffer was able to communicate so powerfully because of these qualities, passed on by a loving father who was not even a man of faith.[7] We would all be wise to practice this discipline in our households, as an expression of our belief.

God created the world and everything in it with His words. We create with ours, too. Speaking words that normalize obscenity, vulgarity, and a lack of reverence for God transform our world, bringing our society into a more negative, God-dishonoring, complaining, and blaming reality. This is completely inconsistent with the values in a culture of virtue. Like the glass of water with dirt added, we can pollute with our mouths a world that is already wading in filth.

Or…like those who defined littering as an offense, we can decide that our spiritual environment is worth saving. We can be the example of clean speech in a world that no longer values it, and set ourselves apart simply by what we don't say, while we take careful account of what we do. We can clear the clouds of polluted speech and thought by speaking words of encouragement and beauty, joy and laughter into a world beaten down with negative journalism, careless talk, and inappropriate innuendo.

---

[7] Metaxas, Eric. *Bonhoeffer: Pastor, Martyr, Prophet, Spy.* Nashville: Thomas Nelson, 2011. Print.

Worthy arguments are made stronger without coarse language. Comedy is funnier when writers look for clever word use instead of curses and sexual slants. Our thinking is elevated when we work within the boundaries of a virtuous imagination and thoughtful, self-controlled communication.

Yes, reality is often graphic. But will we make it moreso, or be part of a culture that celebrates beauty and meaning over vulgar verbalizing? One very practical answer is to begin with the doors of our own mouths.

Questions to Consider and Discuss:

- How might the example of the table with food and bleach apply to all five doors of the heart?

- Has your family discussed and defined vulgarity, cursing, and reverencing God's and Jesus' name?

- What are 20 phrases your family might find encouraging on a day-to-day basis? Write them down and use them accordingly for one week. Note the difference in you and your family members.

- How do you think this door will relate to sexual purity as your child grows?

- What negative phrase from your childhood do you still remember? How about a positive one?

CHILD'S LESSON 5
The Door of the Mouth

Supplies:
- A sports mouthguard

- Healthy food or pictures of it

- A bottle of bleach or other poison, clearly marked

- A puppet, doll, or stuffed animal

- Jellybeans of different flavors

- Lesson 5 downloadable activity page. You will make a face with lips that are open or closed as we learn about using our mouth to help us keep our hearts pure. Memory verse cut-out: Mark 7:15 (NIV). You may also create your own memory card using an index card.

Demonstration

Let everyone try the mouthguard as you explain our need to protect our mouths from accidents. Use washing in between participants as an opportunity to talk about guarding against germs. Ask: If our mouths are a door to our hearts, what should we do? (Watch what we say. What we say can make us clean or dirty.)

The Five Doors of the Heart Activity

Use the heart you made in Lesson 1 to reintroduce the five doors. (Start with all five doors closed, and open them one by one to review the doors of the heart. Then close all doors except the one covering the mouth.) Ask: How do you need to guard your mouth to keep your heart clean? (be careful of the words you use, how you hurt or help people, etc.) Mention that what we eat—what goes into our mouths—doesn't make our hearts dirty, but what we say—what comes out—does. Talk about how we can speak "mud" (negative words) or "bubbles" (positive words). Ask: How does someone feel if we cover him with mud? Bubbles? What are some other examples? Have fun!

Work with your child to color and cut out the downloadable activity page for Lesson 5. Sometimes we should open our mouths, and other times we should keep them shut. Ask: Should you open or close your mouth to say

"Happy Birthday"? To yell at your little brother or sister? To sing a song for Jesus? Talk about several situations, some positive and some negative, and have your child change the mouth to open or closed. Repeat as long as your child is interested.

Book Review
Revisit the page in *The Squire and the Scroll* where the knight shouts at the Squire in the cave. Ask: Why did the knight shout? (He didn't like the boy telling him what to do. He was proud and thought he knew better.) Was it right for him to interrupt the Squire? (No, it was rude, impatient, and prideful.) What happened because he yelled instead of listening? (He didn't hear what the Squire was saying to try to keep him safe, and he turned to stone.) How can we speak words to others to help them do what's right? (Set an example by not using bad language, warn others kindly when they're in danger, tell people God loves them.)

Discussion
Ask: Has anyone ever said anything nasty to you? How did it make you feel? (If it was you, be humble and ask forgiveness.) How does it feel to be called beautiful, handsome, or smart? How would you feel if someone called you "stupid?" Allow your child to describe his/her feelings, like happy, light, like you're flying, like a knife, sad, etc. Explain the power of words to create pain or happiness in yourself and others.

Activity
Do a role play with a puppet, doll, or stuffed animal. Ask: If we call the animal beautiful, how does it feel? (Allow the child to express the feelings of the animal: happy, sad, etc.) Continue to pick words that draw a response, like stupid, ugly, smart, talented, etc. Take a turn yourself and ask the puppet some questions. Have fun! Then ask how your child or a friend might feel if someone said those words to him/her. Would that person feel the same way? Make it clear that words hurt real people in a real way.

Scripture Verse
Look up Matthew 15:11 in your Bible and read it with your child. Make sure he/she understands that what we say, not what we eat, makes our hearts dirty or clean. Define the word "defile."

Snacktime and Prayer

Enjoy jellybeans of different flavors for snacktime. Thank God for all the tastes our mouths can experience, and ask for His help to say only words that are "sweet."

Homeplay

Let your child play with the mouthguard and the mouth activity you made this week, and remind him/her of the lesson you shared. Remind your child that everyone has the choice to close their mouths instead of saying something hurtful or wrong. Show how a mouth can speak "mud" or "bubbles." Read the storybooks again. Recite the child's Scripture verse together once a day, and then try to say it to each other without looking.

5.1 Devotion: The Swinging Door

The Door of the Mouth: Memorize Mark 7:15 (NIV)
Nothing outside a person can defile them by going into them. Rather, it is what comes out of a person that defiles them.

Do not let any unwholesome talk come out of your mouths, but only what is helpful for building others up according to their needs, that it may benefit those who listen. Ephesians 4:29 (NIV)

"We've set a number of standards for healthy eating in our home. But when I think about the fact that what comes out of me defiles me, I recognize that we need to think more about what we're saying than what we're eating."

Our concern for our health can drive us to try new diets, go organic, or count calories. These things aren't bad; in fact, part of parenting is learning to feed our kids the best nutrition we can. It's wise to monitor what goes into our bodies. But the Bible says that's not what makes our hearts impure.

What we say is what makes us fit or unfit spiritually. Our hearts are dirtied by the words that come out of us. The person who speaks peace finds peace themselves, while the person who starts a fight is wounded along with others who get too close.

How do we keep our spirits fit? We guard this door that swings in for food and out for speech. Just as the Squire in *The Squire and the Scroll* knew that he had to be careful about taking *in* the water of the pond, so we have to consider what comes *out* of our mouths. As the water could have made him sick, so our careless, unkind speech can make us sickly Christians.

When we prepare a heart-healthy meal, we think about calories, fats, freshness, and sources. We need similar boundaries with our mouths, thinking before we speak to nourish a healthy spiritual heart.

Will our words bring life or discouragement? Will they bring a smile or sadness? Are they coming from God's Spirit in us, or from a source that could kill, steal, or destroy (see John 10:10)? The answer should determine whether we open or close this swinging door.

How many "calories" of encouragement do you offer your family? Think of positive remarks as an added unit of quality of life. And double bonus: heart condition improves in both the person speaking and the person spoken to!

5.2 Devotion: One Way

The Door of the Mouth: Memorize Mark 7:15 (NIV)
Nothing outside a person can defile them by going into them. Rather, it is what comes out of a person that defiles them.

Out of the same mouth come praise and cursing. My brothers and sisters, this should not be. James 3:10 (NIV)

"One day it's very easy to say positive things, and then another day I do nothing but complain. There may always be ups and downs, but my goal is to become more consistently thankful each day."

Like divisions on a road for fast and slower traffic, our mouths seem to naturally have two lanes. One shoots out all kinds of complaints and sarcastic comments, while the other dispenses encouragement and gratitude.

The goal is to get everything down to one "lane" of thankfulness, worship, and blessings. So how do we start sorting out the traffic of our mouths, shutting down the lane that leads us away from a pure heart?

One way to change our speech is to change what we're focusing on. Ann Voskamp's book, *One Thousand Gifts,* recommends a practice of thankfulness in the form of a journal that simply lists things one is thankful for each day. Entries can include a friend's visit, a flower or bird sighting, an encouraging word, a sweet treat, the color of an apple, or an extra hour of sleep… anything. Our lives are full of unnoticed blessings, and God's will is that we thank Him for them every day (see 1 Thessalonians 5:18).

Our note-taking will then influence our thoughts and speech. When we speak and express our thanks, we open this door of the heart to allow the goodness of our words to nurture ourselves and others. Any good thing we speak of is routed back to bless us personally!

In *The Squire and the Scroll*, the knight showed his gratitude for the Squire's kindly spoken forgiveness by giving over his precious reward. His selfish heart was forever changed by the traffic flowing out of a pure heart. Beautiful events will take place in our hearts and lives too, when we open the door of the mouth to positive comments alone.

Try making a family thankfulness list this week. Just leave a sheet of paper somewhere where anyone can add their gratitude. Catch up at the end of the day or week by reviewing the list and talking about some of what was written. Let thankfulness gain speed as it takes over both lanes!

5.3 Devotion: The Voice of God

The Door of the Mouth: Memorize Mark 7:15 (NIV)
Nothing outside a person can defile them by going into them. Rather, it is what comes out of a person that defiles them.

He lifts his voice, the earth melts. Psalm 46:6 (NIV)

"How do I know when I'm hearing from God? Learning to listen to Him can be a challenge. My prayer is that our family can overcome the noise of this crazy world to enjoy interaction and encouragement from our Father anytime."

God's voice may seem intimidating, but we truly have nothing to fear from Him when we love Him. All God's power is used for our good, and His still, small voice dispenses that power in a sweet, winsome way. God knows how fragile we are, and He converses with us with great sensitivity, forming our hearts with His love.

Opening the door of the mouth to state out loud that God is good, that we love Him, and that we thank and praise Him is an appropriate way to begin. *Our Father which art in heaven, Hallowed be your name* (Matthew 6:9, KJV) is the example Jesus gave. Worship tunes our hearts in to God's unique broadcasting system.

His voice can come to us in the stillness, through the voice of a friend, a Scripture verse, a natural wonder, or a scene in a movie. Our heart may pound. We may cry unexpected tears. We may feel a deep sense of peace or a wave of response within us. Our mind senses that a word or scene is just for us, that God's Spirit is moving in us to reveal a message. We don't "hear" it physically, but we know God is speaking.

The Squire prayed for help and knew God's instruction through a beam of sunlight, a bag of wool, a flower. The Princess received God's comfort through her mother's assurance. We can hear God's loving voice, too.

God's voice is speaking from within us, rewarding our attention with the assurance that He loves us, even rejoicing over us with singing (see Zephaniah 3:17). He is ready to guide and encourage through the impressions we receive as we wait. As we move throughout our days with the awareness that He is there, we find God is constantly interested in us, comforting our hearts with a supernatural peace.

God's voice can be "heard" in many ways. What stories can you tell of God speaking to you or showing you something that revealed His presence? God is always saying He loves us in some way. Draw attention to the everyday messages God sends to you and your family.

5.4 Devotion: Seasoned with Salt

The Door of the Mouth: Memorize Mark 7:15 (NIV)
Nothing outside a person can defile them by going into them. Rather, it is what comes out of a person that defiles them.

Let your conversation be always full of grace, seasoned with salt, so that you may know how to answer everyone. Colossians 4:6 (NIV)

"Good models are rare when it comes to wholesome, polite conversation, so we have to set the example at home. We can always use a little more graciousness in our words!"

A little salt on our food can make a huge difference in taste, and the same is true for our speech. Mary Poppins used a spoonful of sugar to get a similar point across. How we season our words can make all the difference in how they "go down," and how they contribute to a pure heart.

Dry commands are not usually as effective as those couched in loving phrases, accompanied by a tickle or introduced with a bit of comedy, depending on the occasion. A mother who turns on music and a smile to accompany housekeeping will usually get a better response than one who simply gives orders.

God wants us to practice this kind of "seasoning" in all our talk, drawing others in with kindness, courtesy, and laughter. As we close the door of the mouth to sharp commands and speak a welcoming word of encouragement, we show Christ.

This kind of conversation takes time. It can't be managed in barked-out, clipped phrases that direct or refuse to acknowledge. The Princess' mother in the storybook took time to sit in a quiet garden and admire the sky of the Creator as her daughter wrestled with questions of trust. Deep encouragement and comfort resulted from that small investment of time.

We all can practice this kind of communication to help others turn to God and tend to His business. We become instruments of grace as we talk, listen, and speak in a way that brings Jesus' kindness and attentiveness to life (see John 1:14).

Do you introduce requests with compliments, or end heavy discussions with a hug? Think about how you can "season" your words in such a way that even a bitter truth can be received well.

5.5 Devotion: A Spotless Vocabulary

The Door of the Mouth: Memorize Mark 7:15 (NIV)
Nothing outside a person can defile them by going into them. Rather, it is what comes out of a person that defiles them.

One who loves a pure heart and who speaks with grace will have the king for a friend. Proverbs 22:11 (NIV)

"We're working hard to teach our family to be above coarse humor and vulgar talk, to honor God, and to voice opinions intelligently. We want our children to attract friends with those same values."

It's easy to fall in with the crowd and talk the way we hear everyone else talking, to laugh at the same jokes simply because it takes more energy to step away and deal with the funny looks. But if we want a pure heart set apart for God's purposes, we can't be the same as everybody else.

We evidence our uniqueness by using our mouths to express truth, goodness, or beauty. Our speech should be so interesting, so enjoyable, and so clean that we stand out. A parent or child or the President should be able to talk with us without being offended.

That doesn't mean we have to be experts, but we do have to think and practice. Reading the red print in our Bibles gives us a good example of what Jesus spoke. People loved listening to Him talk and tell the parables that were His standard teaching method (see Matthew 13:34).

In *The Princess and the Kiss*, when the farmer came to ask for the Princess' hand, his speech stood out to the young lady and her parents. He didn't brag, boast, or try to seduce their daughter with memorized overtures. He was kind and good, and very courteous, even asking the king and queen's permission to speak. His approach stood out and won him the hand of the Princess, even though he was not of her social status.

Our words work the same way for us. When we guard pure hearts with the way we talk, we too may have kings for friends!

Spotless talk stands out in a world where four-letter words are commonplace. What words or phrases might you remove now from your family vocabulary to bring a new awareness and motivation to guard the heart?

WEEK 6
The Door of the Skin

Lingerie ads. Internet ads. Modern fashion. Confused genders. When it comes to touching, we can get a little nervous, and with good reason. Everything around us seems to be saturated with sexual risk. We hear reports of abuse, pornography, and trafficking, and we naturally fear for our kids.

Breathe for a moment. As we talk about this last door of the heart, recognize that a child's first talks about touch have very little to do with sexuality. But these beginning, basic conversations will help protect and build vital bridges to deeper discussions as a child grows. All the wisdom and practical evaluation you're learning is strengthening your family daily, so take heart!

A common way that we guard our hands is by using an oven mitt. Your child has probably seen one of those in your house often. Our skin's sensitivity to heat, cold, and other sensations requires us to take special care of it. Guarding the skin from extreme temperatures and lacerations is a basic requirement toward caring for our bodies.

When it comes to the skin as a door of the heart, we consider how our hands and feet lead us into places of selfishness or selflessness. What do we take hold of? What paths do our feet take? And how do we choose to touch?

When we teach the Five Doors program in the Dominican Republic, the children learn to say, "No hitting, no kicking, muchos abrazos (many hugs)!" This simple sentence sums up the fact that the door of touch is always for encouragement and help—never for hurting.

Our goal is to help our children understand this at a very basic level. We learned with the door of the breath that life is to be respected. Touch is a way to practice that respect. Touching is not a right, but a privilege. Even when we encourage someone, it may be best to ask, "May I hug you?" The answer is almost always, "Yes!" Still, we show respect toward the other person when we ask. We never know when someone might have been hurt by inappropriate touch, as I learned one day after a radio interview.

I was a member of a Christian band that had been invited to share their story on a local radio station. Out of gratitude, I hugged the lady who interviewed me. I had no idea that she had been abused and hated people touching her. She was so angry that she called and berated me. I apologized and asked her to coffee. Later, she accepted Christ! Touch can be so healing, but now I remember my great friend Beth and ask for permission.

Healthy, safe touch lets our children know what is good. Simple instructions about asking to embrace leads to the important understanding that others must ask to touch us as well. The necessity of a parent or doctor's touch can be differentiated from touching that is forced or invades privacy. A child (or an adult) must always know that their body is their own, and no one can touch them without permission.

Encourage and model healthy touch in your child's presence. Hugs and simple kisses between spouses model a happy married life, and hands held around the table in prayer show the precious communion of the family and between believers. Appropriate touch is powerful in conjunction with prayer for the sick or hurting. It's said that we all need about eight hugs a day to be well, so don't be stingy. You and others' emotional health is at stake!

Grocery shopping is a great time to learn and teach about touch in terms of what we pick up. What do we truly need, and what do we simply want? In a materialistic society, we can grab almost anything we like, but should we? Are we buying needlessly or selfishly? After filling our grocery basket, we can place a couple of items in a box for the needy, or buy a candy bar for the check-out clerk to make his day, or leave a few extra dollars to help pay for the family behind us.

Our hands are meant for giving, not hoarding. Opening our hands to give at least as often as we receive opens this door to generosity and sharing, and shapes all hearts involved for a lifetime. Small incidents of kindness like this are what children remember and often practice in their own families later on.

Finally, it's wise to include a focus on where our feet take us as we guard the door of touch. Think in terms of what paths of life are rough or smooth, wise or foolish. The Squire had a tricky problem with this door in *The Squire and the Scroll* when he found boots to wear for a slippery path. We will often find ways that seem right to us, but we will need God to show us which paths are absolutely safe.

In all aspects of this door, God can direct us when emotions run high or thoughts are whirling in our heads. Though the door of touch may seem intimidating, God will never fail to lead us if we ask. With His help we can manage this door, or any door, in ourselves and our families with wisdom and grace.

Questions to Consider and Discuss:

- When you think of the sense of touch, how do you react? Talk about your fears or responses.

- Explain good touch and bad touch out loud and very briefly, as if you were talking to your child. This is a practice exercise. Share some ideas with your group and give each other input. (You can practice with a friend for any type of discussion, anytime!)

- Is materialism a problem in your household? What are some ways to encourage giving over receiving?

- Where are your feet taking you right now? Are your steps worthy of followers?

- How comfortable is your family with affection? Is there room for more development in the practice of encouraging touch? How?

- Have you sought help for any issues with touch you experience yourself?

CHILD'S LESSON 6
The Door of the Skin

Supplies:
- An oven mitt
- A blindfold and items (not displayed, but hidden for activity time) that are soft, hard, rough, smooth, hot, and cold (Examples: furry stuffed animal or coat, small board, sandpaper, paper, warm blanket, ice cube)
- Marshmallows and hard candy
- Lesson 6 downloadable activity page. You will make a paper doll with clothes to put on and off as we learn about protecting our skin to help us keep our hearts pure. Memory verse cut-out: Ecclesiastes 3:1, 5 (NIV). You may also create your own memory card using an index card.

Demonstration

Let everyone take turns wearing the oven mitt as you explain our need to protect our skin from burns. Ask: If touch is a door to our hearts, what should we do? (Touch in a way that helps and doesn't hurt.)

The Five Doors of the Heart Activity

Use the heart you made in Lesson 1 to reintroduce the five doors. (Start with all five doors closed, and open them one by one to review the doors of the heart. Then close all doors except the one covering the hand.) Ask: How do you think you need to guard your skin to keep your heart clean? (not hitting or kicking; hugging instead, etc.). Talk about how we can appropriately touch to make others feel better or to show love. Mention why asking permission before we touch is important (some people have been hurt by touch). Make it clear that your child has power over his or her own body, and no one else is allowed to touch him/her without permission.

Work with your child to color and cut out the downloadable activity page for Lesson 6. Ask: What are some important ways that we protect our skin from harm? Have your child place each piece of clothing on the paper doll where it belongs. Then tell how that clothing is offering protection to the body. Repeat as long as your child is interested.

Book Review

Revisit the page in *The Princess and the Kiss* where the farmer asks the parents' permission just to talk to the Princess. Ask: Why is this important?

(The Princess was so special that he wanted to show extra respect to her and her parents.) Now go to the page in *The Squire and the Scroll* where the Squire chooses a path. Ask: What happened? Why was the Squire a little confused? How did the boots help him decide where to go? Remind your child that God will always help us to decide where to go and will keep us from danger.

Discussion

Ask: Have you ever been physically hurt by someone? How did it make you feel? (Sad? Unloved?) How does it feel to be hugged? Now take some time to hug each other, slowly. Hold each other for twenty seconds or longer if at all possible. Ask: How did this hug feel? (Don't be surprised if tears are shed.) Ask: Would you like to have a hug like this every day? Give your child permission to ask for one if you forget. Talk about the important feeling of safety that a family can give when they show each other love this way. Ask: What other ways can you show loving touch? (Kisses, high fives, silly wrestling, holding hands during prayer, touching a shoulder, etc.) Tell your child what to do if someone ever touches him/her in a way that hurts or makes him/her feel bad. (Tell you or another named, trusted adult RIGHT AWAY no matter what the other person says. Remind your child that you will always protect him/her. Warn against being alone with a stranger or anyone who makes him/her feel uncomfortable. Make sure your child knows to RUN and TELL, no matter what!)

Activity

Take turns blindfolding each other and feeling the different surfaces from the supply list with your bare feet, naming what you feel and noticing how your skin "reads" objects of different textures (some objects may give more than one sensation).

Scripture Verse

Look up Ecclesiastes 3:1, 5 (NIV) in your Bible and read it with your child: *There is a time for everything…a time to embrace, and a time to refrain from embracing.* Ask: What does "refrain" mean? Talk about times that are right for hugging and other times when it may not be a good idea.

Snacktime and Prayer

Have everyone close their eyes before snacktime. Hand each person a marshmallow and an unwrapped hard candy or lollipop (it can be smooth or rough as well). See if each person can guess what the snacks are. Ask: What does your sense of touch tell you?

Homeplay

Let your child play with the oven mitt, textured objects, and the paper doll you made this week, and remind them of what they learned. Remind your child that she has the choice to hug instead of hitting or kicking. Show her how kicking should only involve a ball (or karate, if your child is involved). Remind your child that a hand is for giving and helping (open hand), not hitting or taking (fist). Place the candy in the open hand to show giving and under the fist to show selfishness. Talk about how our feet can take us to dangerous or safe places. Read the storybooks again. Recite the Scripture verse together once a day, and then try to say it to each other without looking.

6.1 Devotion: Physical Praise

The Door of the Skin: Memorize Ecclesiastes 3:1, 5 (NIV)
*There is a time for everything…a time to embrace
and a time to refrain from embracing.*

Therefore I want the men everywhere to pray, lifting up holy hands without anger or disputing. 1 Timothy 2:8 (NIV)

"We want to see our children busy and involved in worship and prayer. Nothing is better than seeing them reaching out to Jesus and others!"

Using the hands and body specifically for acts of worship is a sacrifice of praise that produces unique fruit. Nothing is quite like the physical expression of praise, which is mentioned often in the Bible and shapes the heart deeply. If we can express our excitement at a football game, surely there's reason to consider a physical response to the God of the universe!

Too often we relegate physical expression and hand motion to our children, but Jesus makes it clear that we must be like little children to enter the kingdom of heaven (see Matthew 18:3). Our "dignity" as adults can turn into pride that hardens our hearts against God.

Why not open the door of the skin to using our hands as instruments of praise instead? Why not hold hands when praying? Why not put our hands on someone when we're praying for them? Why not kneel? Why not dance? These practices can certainly contribute to keeping our hearts childlike and pure.

In the storybook, when the Squire held up his scroll before the dragon, he was physically making a statement that God's wisdom would defend and protect him, and his bold declaration brought the defeat of the evil beast. Such declarations in praise and prayer in our own lives can build boldness, courage, and faith, strengthening us to resist the enemy and flee from him (see James 4:7).

Challenge yourself to risk a greater expression in worship, and let your child express himself, too. Gentle guidance can be appropriate, but be more eager to learn than to correct. Don't put out the flame of desire for God that can so naturally arise through our hands and bodies. Open the door of the skin to physical worship!

Families and churches worship differently, but our personal expression and obedience to God should not feel restrained by manmade rules. Evaluate your family's worship in church and at home. What new opportunities can you take to allow each other to express physically your adoration of the Lord?

6.2 Devotion: Open Arms

The Door of the Skin: Memorize Ecclesiastes 3:1, 5 (NIV)
*There is a time for everything…a time to embrace
and a time to refrain from embracing.*

She opens her arms to the poor and extends her hands to the needy.
Proverbs 31:20 (NIV)

"Our whole family can be whiny and grabby when we're shopping. It's time to do less shopping and more reaching out. Giving provides so much more joy than getting!"

In the Bible, James tells us that caring for orphans and widows is true religion (see James 1:27). Like the Proverbs 31 woman, we're all required to open our hands and arms to the poor and needy. This contributes greatly to opening the door of the skin to compassionate acts of going and giving. And reaching out is a great adventure!

Serving others daily requires intentionality and a willingness to allow our schedule to be interrupted. Opportunities are all around, but we must develop and model a willingness to go out of our way, expect the unexpected, and plan to serve. This welcoming of adventure and discovery connects with our children, and especially connects with our boys as they develop into servant leaders who fight injustice.

As the Squire humbly served the king and the knight, we bow our knee to serve the homeless and the needy. As our children see us hand a bag of supplies out the window, visit a friend in a nursing home, or take a meal to someone sick, they grow in compassion themselves.

Open your heart to unexpected opportunities to help someone today. Take your child with you, talk about how you served, or ask your child to help you prepare needed supplies. Hearts that serve strangers will someday serve their own families as well.

Perform one planned act of service with your family this week, and look out for one unexpected opportunity (at least). Work up to two per week, then three per week, and keep going!

6.3 Devotion: God's Righteous Hand

The Door of the Skin: Memorize Ecclesiastes 3:1, 5 (NIV)
*There is a time for everything…a time to embrace
and a time to refrain from embracing.*

I will strengthen you and help you; I will uphold you with my righteous right hand. Isaiah 41:10 (NIV)

"Sometimes the whole issue of purity seems so overwhelming, and everything that has to do with touch intimidates me. I haven't lived my life perfectly, and I don't know how to teach my children what I didn't do myself. I need God's help!"

Every parent needs God's help to pursue purity and teach it. We're in good company when it comes to pursuing pure hearts!

God's right hand is strong toward us when we need Him. According to the Bible, God's right hand upholds us (see Psalm 63:8), holds treasures for us (see Psalm 16:11), is full of righteousness (see Psalm 48:10), saves (see Psalm 20:6), provides a place of refuge (see Psalm 17:7), is strong (see Psalm 89:13), and shatters the enemy (see Exodus 15:6), just to mention a few.

The main goal, overall, is to acknowledge God, thank Him, and trust Him. When we surrender our lives to Him, He is faithful to form our hearts, even in our imperfection. Even better, He gives us His righteousness so that we can operate as He would, choosing to open and close the door of the skin at the right times. The grace He provided on the cross covers all our failure, past and present. So how can we lose? God has us covered.

Don't forget that the One who is in you is greater than the one who is in the world (see 1 John 4:4), and that He's made you more than a conqueror (see Romans 8:37), *no matter your past.* He's thrown that stuff as far as the east is from the west (see Psalm 103:12).

So relax and enjoy building a culture of virtue in your family, whether you do it in the context of something you share when you're feeling strong, or whether you teach in the midst of a painful moral failure. Jesus died for this imperfect world. He died for you and your child. God's righteous right hand covers you and your heart.

Your child is in your house because you're the right parent for him or her! When it comes to good opportunities for learning, failures work just as well, or better, than successes. Next time you experience something that seems like a failure, ask God to show you how it can become an opportunity to learn or teach.

6.4 Devotion: Hardworking Hands

The Door of the Skin: Memorize Ecclesiastes 3:1, 5 (NIV)
*There is a time for everything…a time to embrace
and a time to refrain from embracing.*

The hand of the diligent will rule, while the slothful will be put to forced labor. Proverbs 12:24 (ESV)

"I'm not sure many people today understand the benefits of hard work. I want my kids to tackle tough jobs without complaining. That will benefit them and others no matter what they do."

Knowing how to work hard and cheerfully may seem to be a lost art, but it's more valuable than ever. Employers constantly search for people who know how to complete tough tasks and be pleasant while they're doing so. A great attitude toward work is evidence of a pure heart.

Most of us don't live on farms these days, and our kids are spending more time with computers and phones than mops and shovels. This loss of physical work and responsibility makes families more stressed. Whining ensues more easily, even with the smallest task, when a family is sitting down too much.

But life is ahead, and life requires work, so it's best to give our kids work often. Of course, if we want them to have a cheerful attitude, we need to set that example as well. If Mom and Dad complain about working, children probably will too. Opening the door of the skin to work can become a joyful gift to the Lord (see Colossians 3:23).

In *The Princess and the Kiss*, the suitor the Princess chose was a farmer. He didn't go to the gym, or learn great pick-up lines, or financially strategize to become a millionaire. He worked hard. And the king and queen saw something in his heart that they didn't see in the others. In fact, they thought enough of this man to allow him to become part of their royal family!

Our children will have great hearts and opportunities too, if they can work hard and with a good attitude. Get your family started on some purposeful activity today!

What is the attitude about work in your household? Consider having a go-to list of chores and more physical activities that need to be completed before "screen time." Everyone can benefit from less time on screen and more time in action!

6.5 Devotion: Hands That God Loves

The Door of the Skin: Memorize Ecclesiastes 3:1, 5 (NIV)
*There is a time for everything...a time to embrace
and a time to refrain from embracing.*

*There are six things the L*ORD *hates, seven that are detestable to him: haughty eyes, a lying tongue, hands that shed innocent blood, a heart that devises wicked schemes, feet that are quick to rush into evil, a false witness who pours out lies and a person who stirs up conflict in the community.* Proverbs 6:16-18 (NIV)

"It's good to know that I'm building up to discussions about sexuality by starting with teaching my kids about a pure heart. That will connect to the more intimate talks and make them easier to approach as they get older."

Hands should always help, hearts should plan to help, and feet should run from evil. When we look at Proverbs 6:16-18, we can steer clear of the things God hates and do what He loves instead. That's exactly the choice that makes and guards a pure heart.

Learning how to help, how to plan to do good, and how to run toward God and away from sin are practices that we will develop for a lifetime, applying them in different ways during different stages of our lives. Your children need simple guidance to use self-control and make good choices now, but these seemingly small corrections are vital foundation stones for sexual integrity in the coming years.

The five simple rules on the Squire's scroll are an example of the basic rules of biblical living and reflect the simplicity of the Ten Commandments. The Squire's parents taught these simple rules as he grew, and look at the man he became! We can instill basic but powerful values of help, rescue, honor, respect, goodness, truth, and beauty in our children as well. This will lay a firm foundation for all of life ahead.

Don't obsess over the "important" talks you will have with your child in the future. The basics of the Five Doors you're teaching right now are every bit as important. Train your family's hands to do good and their feet to run to God. Every ounce of effort in this direction is contributing to their pursuit of purity in heart and body.

Your child's years from 6-12 are so important in teaching him/her all the rock-solid values that will contribute to success on every level. Congratulate yourself on being tuned in to your child's needs right now and taking them seriously! You are one of those rare parents who is changing the world by devoting yourself to a culture of virtue!

TECHNOLOGY AGREEMENT

Important Note: *DO NOT feel you must use these guidelines. This example is given only as a starting point. Consider each point in light of your individual family situation and child. Be very intentional in reviewing each boundary, then introduce the agreement with a friendly but businesslike meeting. Enforce your "guard rails" with confidence.*

Our Priorities:
- God
- Family
- Work/School
- Friends

Facebook:
- No social networking without Mom and Dad's access. If we don't have the password, it shouldn't exist.
- NO obscenity. If someone sends obscenity, immediately delete it and block the person if it continues.
- Photos must be appropriate. No cleavage, sexy poses, unnecessary posing with girlfriends, bra straps, and so on. If you are in doubt, leave it out.
- Limit the number of photos on your Facebook. Limit 15 events with 20 pictures each. Choose the best, leave the rest.
- Limit the number of friends to 110 plus family and mentors.
- Applications must be appropriate. Check with Mom and Dad as needed.
- Remember, Mom and Dad will be checking pages regularly. If we ask you to remove something, the instruction should be received with a good attitude.
- Time limits: half hour segments. Use your time wisely.

Phone:
- No sending pictures unless to parents or siblings.

- Purposeful texting. Limit "What's up?" "I don't know. What's up with you?" types of interaction.

- Purposeful calling. Time limits for boy/girl conversation. No calls after 9:30 p.m. unless approved by Mom or Dad.

- No phone calls at the table or during family time (including car time or family trips in the car, and so on).

Discipline:
- Three warnings will be issued for a negative attitude in following these guidelines. Upon the third warning, the device involved will be off limits for 24 hours. Days will be added for further infractions.